# Exotic Asian Cooking

Complete production: Naumann & Göbel Verlagsgesellschaft mbH, Cologne
Printed in Poland


ISBN 3-625-11087-3

# Exotic Asian Cooking

NAUMANN & GÖBEL

# PREFACE

Asian cooking is more than just a mixture of strange ingredients – Asian cooking is a cultural and culinary adventure!

Looking back on a few millennia, we would like to introduce you to a culinary tradition where eating is understood to be more than just a mere necessity – it is a harmonic interaction between cooking and culture.

Even though the Far East has elements that remain forever mysterious and unknown to our Western eyes, the main maxim of its cuisine is surprisingly simple: after a meal you should feel satisfied and at peace. This, however, is only possible if the food is well balanced, i.e. if the ingredients harmonise in taste and texture. What the "Nouvelle Cuisine" rediscovers today was part and parcel of an Asian cook's knowledge already 2,000 years ago:

- use fresh produce in season
- keep cooking times short
- use the right spices.

The colonial era, wars and, last but not least, mass tourism all have contributed to changing Asian eating habits. One idea that has remained, however, is the principle of balance.

On the following pages you will find a lot of interesting information on Asian countries, the continent's peoples, their cooking, eating habits and culture – and of course recipes which you can vary time and again as the mood takes you.

"... May the rice gently escort the fish, meat, poultry and vegetables to your stomach..."

Let this flowery invitation – which simply means "Bon Appétit" – put you in the mood for our great culinary adventure.

# CONTENTS

## Cooking and Culture – The Secret of the Asian Cuisine

In the case of Asian cuisine one cannot talk about cooking and culture as two separate entities. They are more a combination of one and the same resulting in a culinary culture or an art form, developed and perfected over thousands of years. One could even say that it is absolutely unique in this world. Famous scholars spent their lives looking for the perfect balance and harmony in Asian dishes.

The apparently simple Asian cuisine is based on just such knowledge of dietary correlations and effects.

For Asians it is of little importance how you eat something. The emphasis lies in what you eat and especially why you eat it.

This philosophy paved the way for the rich variety, the imaginative, spicy, appetising and light cuisine we know today – a cuisine that does not tax the stomach.

Discover with us the secrets of the Asian kitchen, cooking and culture. We will start right in the heart of the continent.

## The Culinary Regions

### Chinese Cuisine

The Chinese cuisine belongs to the best in the world and has played a dominant role in shaping Asian cooking. Because of the country's size and its cherished culinary tradition it is among the most varied and attractive of its kind. Only a few years ago "sweet and sour" was commonly regarded as a prototypical feature of the Chinese cuisine – at least in the eyes of a Westerner. This was due to Asian cooks merging Far Eastern and Western cuisines in the hope of increasing turnover. Nowadays, however, a true culinary culture worth its salt can be found outside of China. Chinese cooking is simpler than you think. The ingredients should be carefully selected and prepared; you will need subtle seasoning and a good helping of imagination. This is easier said than done. It is only practice that makes you master Chinese cooking (says Confucius), but then you will work wonders (say we). You do not need any special kitchen equipment and only those ingredients you will be able to obtain from well stocked Asian shops.

The diversity of the Chinese countryside is matched by the variety of regional cuisines. There are no real borders. We therefore decided on splitting Chinese cuisine into Northern, Southern, Eastern and Western varieties because this has reasonably pronounced differences. The North is China's oldest region, steeped in history. It is not, however, blessed with many natural resources. The climate is rough, the land fallow. However, even such conditions did not prevent a good, nutritious, down-to-earth cuisine from developing. The staple food is not rice like in other parts of China, but millet and wheat. This cuisine has also benefited from Mongolian influences. What these so-called barbarians cooked on their shields over a camp-fire was later refined by Northern Chinese chefs and turned into the world-famous Mongolian Hot Pot.

This region has also given rise to another dish that is well known throughout the world – the Peking Duck. Often copied, this dish makes every gourmet go weak at the knees at the thought of this crispy piece of bird.

Westerners can get to grips with the Northern Chinese cuisine relatively quickly, because we are used to ingredients such as meat, freshwater fish, poultry and vegetables. The main seasonings consist of spring onions, garlic and ginger – used to good effect rather than in great quantities.

The difference between the Northern and Southern styles of cooking is greater than just the change of climate. The region is blessed with arable land of the best quality and an ideal climate for growing rice and vegetables. It has a long coastline and the sea is seething with fish and seafood. All you need is creative and imaginative cooks – and the variety of possible combinations is endless. Both the palate and the eye are in for a real treat. The dishes are decorated so perfectly that one nearly does not dare destroy the little works of art.

Eastern Chinese cuisine is a successful mixture between its Northern and Southern cousins. Pork, chicken, vegetables and especially fish and seafood form the basis for delicate and aromatic dishes. One of the main aims is to enhance the ingredients' flavours with subtle seasoning. It is here that red cooking – a style also well known in our culture – has its origins.

China's West is home to the chilli pepper – that small pod which looks quite innocuous but is in fact devilishly hot. Its frequent use in Western Chinese cooking has two good reasons. Not only does it add flavour, but the humid and hot climate in that part of the country means that fresh foodstuffs do not keep for long. This is precisely where the chilli pepper comes in handy. It kills off germs, cleans the intestines and because it makes one perspire it purifies the body. The range of flavours you encounter in Western China, however, extend from very hot all the way to fragrantly sweet. This is due partly to the manifold variety of dishes and partly to the powerfully fragrant spices that make the taste buds specially sensitive.

**Japanese Cuisine**

One could almost call the Japanese cuisine "spiritualized". The Japanese's special feeling for nuances and subtleties is not only reflected in their art and everyday life, but also in the kitchen and at the dinner table. The freshness and untampered state of the ingredients is emphasized by their remarkable plainness and simplicity. This should not be taken to mean, however, that Japanese food is boring or dull. The apparent simplicity is much more an expression of understated elegance, similar to that found in Japanese gardens, theatres or in a Bonsai tree. "The dish should always enhance the nature of its ingredients..." – this is how a chef described the essence of Japanese cuisine.

Even though China's influence on Japanese culture and language is irrefutable, Japanese cuisine lacks the luxuriance and variety of its Chinese cousin. The reasons are both of a religious and a geographical nature. Japan is not only much smaller, but also offers entirely different natural habitats. Its inhabitants have to cope with what the land has to offer. Insularity accounts for the almost complete lack of foreign influences (the only exception being tea which – after having been consumed in China for some time – was considered sufficiently noble a drink to refresh the Japanese palate from the 12th century onwards). Rice and fish continue to this day to be the staple foodstuffs. This is because Japan lacks arable land but has plenty of coastline. The "People of the Divine Wind" have been pursuing the goal of alimentary self-sufficiency with a similar eagerness which they displayed when they embraced industrialization. The astonishing result is that the production of rice, fruit, vegetables and meat nearly meets the country's demand.

**Korea**

Korea is situated between China and Japan. The Koreans have more or less voluntarily adapted aspects of the cuisines of its two neighbouring superpowers. But smaller nations can be quite pigheaded when they put their minds to it and so the Koreans managed to create to an imaginative, nourishing and very respectable cuisine of their own.

It is comprised of nutritious soups, spicy rice dishes with meat and vegetables as well as imaginative fish and seafood specialities. A side dish the Korean simply cannot do without is "kimchi", a spicy cold accompaniment made from fermented vegetables such as cabbage, radish, turnips, garlic, cucumber, spinach, leek, soy beans, onions, chilli and ginger. Vegetables in season get pickled, placed in an earthenware pot and stored in a cool place. This is, however, about the only similarity between Korean cooking and the Central European sauerkraut!

**Thailand**

The whole of Thailand appears to be a huge, beautifully fragrant kitchen. Wherever you go you will come across food – either raw, on the plentiful, sweet smelling markets, or already cooked and enticingly arranged at one of the countless street corner stalls. Rice is a staple foodstuff in Thailand. But because of nature's overflowing larder it is not just any old rice, but special fragrant Thai rice. Side dishes are plentiful and there is something for every palate and taste – ranging from sweet to spicy hot. And the best thing is: they serve to stimulate your appetite so that you want more. A perhaps surprising fact is that the Thai do not eat with chopsticks: they prefer a spoon and fork. The latter is used to pile the food onto the spoon, which inciden-

tally is a European import. But the spoon is not the only element the Thai have borrowed from other cultures. Influences from their Asian neighbours have been skilfully incorporated into the Thai cuisine. This has made it one of the most colourful fares of the Asian continent.

## The Philippines, Malaysia and Indonesia

The Asian island states of the Philippines, Malaysia and Indonesia have a culinary culture that successfully and imaginatively integrates a multitude of different cuisines to come up with a new and attractive variety of dishes. The Philippine cuisine, apart from the Chinese and Japanese influences, has also taken on board some Spanish and Portuguese habits. You will even find a kind of siesta after a meal and herbs such as oregano and bay leaves. In Malaysia too you will come across Chinese, Indian and Portuguese herbs and spices. However, you would eat with you fingers – a practice which, if done skilfully, is just as elegant as eating with a knife and fork. First you roll the rice into little balls using the first three fingers of your right hand. You then dip these balls into whichever dish before placing in your mouth. Serving food on banana leaves is not only very pretty, but also environmentally friendly. Last but not least – it also saves you doing the washing up!

## Indonesian Cuisine

One of the most famous Indonesian dishes is the rice table – and it does give a fair estimation of what you can expect if you delve deeper into the subject. Indonesian cuisine reflects the whole colourful kaleidoscope of the world of cooking and manages to represent all its flavours. You will find every little nuance – from the mildest coconut dish right through to the spicy hot sambal. And one must not forget the delicious Indonesian spices, whose enticing flavours made it all the way to Europe, enthusing the Dutch as the first Europeans for some 200 years now.

## Laos, Cambodia, Vietnam

The different cooking styles of Laos, Cambodia and, albeit to a lesser degree, Vietnam are little known in the West. The people in these countries eat rice, venison, game, mushrooms, poultry and many freshwater fish. Edible leaves and pods enrich the list of vegetables while wild herbs are used for seasoning. Sometimes one can discern Chinese and, from colonial times, French influences. In Vietnam, however, things are different. An attractive and quite idiosyncratic cuisine developed. Initial Western touches provided by the French did not survive the colonialists' stay and disappeared again soon after they had left. All that remains are perhaps coffee and French bread sticks. The Vietnamese are true artists when it comes to wrapping food. This is done painstakingly and lovingly with lettuce, vegetable or edible rice paper leaves. Not only does it look nice, but it is practical at the same time, as the Vietnamese use neither chopsticks nor knife and fork, but their hands to dip the parcels into a variety of different sauces. Only in the case of soup is a spoon in order and chopsticks are used for the more solid ingredients. Apart from the numerous leafy vegetables, herbs such as dill, fennel, basil, coriander and mint are worth mentioning, as they are all well known to the European cook, too.

## Indian Cuisine

The Indian subcontinent is a country of extremes. Geographically you have the highlands with snow all year round in the North while at the same time in the South you will encounter tropical palms. In social terms you have a strict caste system with a near lack of the middle classes leaving only the very rich and the very poor. On the cultural side of things you have many different peoples all with their own religious background and different loyalties that influence their day-to-day lives.

From these apparent contradictions and some foreign influences, the Indians have created a cuisine full of compromises that is very varied and full of surprises. Despite regional differences they share one common passion: the curry. This has little to do with the yellowish powder we know in the West that lends every meal that typical "Indian" flavour. Curry is much more the Indian national dish. Carefully selected ingredients and spices form the basis of every good curry. To an Indian cook the term "well-seasoned" does not stand for one predominant taste, but rather a felicitous combination of four different types of flavours. This is why a curry does not always have to be spicy hot. It can also be a mild dish with the merest hint of different flavours. The most famous Indian spices bar onions and garlic are aniseed, chilli, curcuma, cumin, coriander, cardamom, ginger and cinnamon. And while we are on the subject it is just as well to straighten out one further misapprehension. The Indians are not a vegetarian people. It goes without saying that the different regions do influence the national cuisine but more often than not it is economic pressures rather than religious fervour that lead a person to becoming a vegetarian.

## CULINARY SUBTLETIES

### Herbs and Spices

Only those who, like the Asians, delve into the reasons of why people eat what they eat will be able to season properly. This is easier said than done. It entails not only adding flavours to those already provided by your ingredients, but to increase your appetite, stimulate digestion and the cardiovascular system as well as kill off bacteria – in short to prepare food in such a manner that it tastes great and is beneficial to your body at the same time. This brings us once again to the maxim of a balanced diet and what an important role herbs and spices have to play in this concept.

Already in the 7th century A.D. Chinese herbalists could concoct potions and dietary plans that astound Western scientists to this day. The notion that you can combat a great many illnesses with food alone must have been worth its salt since the innovator of this theory lived to the ripe old age of more than one hundred years! And this at a time when the average life expectancy lay somewhere between 25 to 30 years.

Herbs and spices have always had a special pull on people. Even more so when they stem from the Far East – a place that still carries with it a mysterious flair for most Westerners and one that had remained more or less closed to Western civilisation for a very long time. One can therefore imagine the sensation caused by reports of spice islands, paradises of odours and colours. No wonder that people were prepared to pay the most outrageous amounts of money to enjoy these delicacies!

Many a European merchant family became wealthy because of the Asian spice trade.

These days getting hold of Asian herbs and spices is somewhat easier. Well-stocked specialized shops and supermarkets have adapted to recent trends and offer many exotic ingredients. In case you have never heard of one or the other wort mentioned in this book have a look at the information below.

### Chilli

You can get chilli either fresh or dried. Be careful, the pods are so hot that you ought to wear gloves when handling or cutting them. It is the seeds that are responsible for the hotness of these little devils – a fact that is shared by all plants of this family.

### Spring Onions

Spring onions are milder than their normal small or large counterparts. Do not let the word "spring" mislead you into thinking that these onions only grow during that season. Actually, you can get them all year round. The name refers much more to the green and tender appearance.

### Curry Powder

Curry is a mixture of spices. Asian cooks mix different curry depending on taste, occasion and ingredients. The five flavours – namely sweet, sour, bitter, mild and hot – must harmonize. If you want to recreate this you should roast dried spices such as cardamom, cumin, curcuma, pepper, cinnamon, cloves, chilli and mace in a frying pan without any oil or butter. Careful: they burn easily! Leave them to cool down before grinding with a pestle and mortar. You can keep your curry powderin well sealed jars for a limited period.

### Ginger

Ginger, more than any other spice, is quite simply the Asian seasoning per se. Already the great philosopher Confucius prepared all his dishes using ginger – and if anybody knew, then him. The yellowish brown, bizarrely shaped roots contain substances that stimulate the digestive system and kill off bacteria. Use fresh ginger whenever possible. It is much tastier than its ground counterpart and you will be able to taste the whole range of flavours on offer from aromatic to spicy hot.

## Cardamom

The taste of cardamom is reminiscent of cloves and cinnamon. It is the seeds of this evergreen perennial belonging to the ginger family that are used for seasoning our dishes. They are not only aromatic, however, but also possess medicinal properties. As such they stimulate the digestive system and also display antiseptic qualities.

## Cumin

Cumin looks pretty similar to our own caraway seed and its stimulating effects on our digestive system are also comparable. The taste, however, is quite different so that these two seasonings are not always interchangeable. If you would like to find out how cumin tastes you ought to try a digestive liqueur where it is often one of the main ingredients.

## Pimento

These are the dried berries of an evergreen myrtle tree. Their taste can be placed somewhere between cloves and peppercorns, which is why it is sometimes also known as clove pepper. They should be either be used whole or crushed before cooking. Other names include allspice, myrtle pepper or Jamaican pepper. Pimento is commonly used in conjunction with bay leaves to poach fish and meats.

## Coriander

Also called "Chinese parsley". The only thing these two herbs have in common, however, is their appearance. Their tastes are quite different. Asian cuisine uses the whole plant: the aromatic leaves, the peppercorn sized seeds (either whole or ground) whose flavour is reminiscent of cinnamon and nutmeg as well as the roots. The annual will grow in any herb garden without causing any fuss.

## Nutmeg and Mace

Nutmeg and mace stem from the same tree. Mace is the thin, bright red aril or lace-like covering over the shell of the walnut sized nutmeg. You will get most out of the nut's aromatic bitter flavour if you grate it fresh. Mace on the other hand is added whole or roughly chopped but should be removed prior to serving.

## Saffron and Curcuma

Saffron and curcuma add colour to your dish rather than taste. Saffron stems from the dried yellow stigmas of the violet flowers of a crocus plant. It is a very expensive spice and has been known in the West for a relatively long time to add both flavour and colour to dishes and soups. Curcuma lends curry powder its yellow colour and is a considerably cheaper substitute for saffron not only for us in the West but also in Asia. It is also said to clean the blood.

**Star-Anise**

Star-anise – as the name suggests – actually resembles little stars and smells of aniseed. It can be replaced with either aniseed itself or with fennel seeds.

**Lemon Grass**

This grass usually found in marshes and swamps really does taste of lemons. You only use the thick, white bulbous bottom parts. Well-stocked supermarkets or Asian food shops will have it fresh if you are lucky, but getting hold of it dried should not pose any problems. Recently, a ground version has come onto the market, too. However, should you not be successful in your search you can always use finely grated lemon zest.

## Rice and Noodles

Asian food without rice would be like the seaside without the sea. A meal without rice is utterly unthinkable. This oldest of cultivated plants must be quite special in one way or another if you take into account that almost half the human population have made it their staple food. It might have something to do with "inner values" because the plant's appearance is after all quite unspectacular. It's taste can best be described as neutral not to put too fine a point on it. But it is exactly this quality that makes it the ideal accompaniment to the already well seasoned Asian meat, fish and vegetable dishes. The flowery language of the Far East puts it beautifully: "Rice accompanies other food to the stomach in the most agreeable manner..."

It is only a recent trend that rice is getting more attention in the West, too. Even here we have discovered the life-giving qualities each little grain carries within: vitamins, minerals, carbohydrates, trace elements, fibre and plenty of easily digestible proteins. Moreover, rice is quickly and easily prepared, there is no limit to what you can do with it and it is filling without taxing the digestive system. The roughly 8,000 different kinds of rice can be classed according to their appearance: long grain, medium grain and short grain rice.

Long grain rice – as the name suggests – has a long, narrow and quite hard core. Cooked, it stays nice and dry and does not get clotted. The most famous of its kind is patna rice, available both in a brown and a parboiled version. The latter should by right have lost most of its nutrients if it were not for a special technique which preserves all the goodness normally lost during the finishing process of grinding and polishing. A special Asian delicacy is the basmati or fragrant rice. It will make your mouth water as soon as you put it on the hob!

Medium and short grain rice are not only shorter and rounder in appearance, but also have a softer inside than their long grained counterparts. They are the favourite of those nations that eat with chopsticks. The reasons for this are obvious. The cooked grains are quite dry and fluffy, but will stick together so that you can easily pick out a dollop using chopsticks without half of your portion falling off again – or even worse, go to waste. By the way, cooking rice is not nearly as complicated as it seems. In this book we always use the Chinese way of cooking it. That way success is guaranteed each and every time and it is terribly simple:

Transfer two cups of dry rice into a saucepan. Pour in three cups of water, add salt to taste and bring everything to the boil. As soon as it boils, turn down the flame and leave to simmer until the rice has absorbed all the water. Once this is accomplished you end up with five cups of delicious and perfectly cooked rice.

Noodles enjoy a similar popularity to rice in Asian cooking. In some regions they have even tipped the little grains to becoming the staple food. However, not even there did they manage to replace rice completely – instead they contain rice flour. Noodles come in a number of different varieties. Made from rice flour they are very thin and nearly transparent when raw. They are dried in bundles and usually fried. Others are made of wheat flour with or without eggs. So-called glass noodles are also available and are made of bean flour. These are quite similar to rice noodles in that they are very thin and almost transparent. One should not cook them either but pour boiling water over them as otherwise they will disintegrate and stick together in clumps. When you fry these noodles, however, they become nice and fluffy and just a little crispy.

Wheat and egg noodles come in all shapes and sizes: broad and narrow ribbon noodles, very thin vermicelli or of medium thickness similar to spaghetti.

## Cooking Utensils and Techniques

The most famous Asian cooking utensil is the wok. This Chinese pan is simply fantastic. Its design is timeless, the material it is made of is very tough and extremely energy efficient. The latter characteristic was an important consideration when cooking utensils were designed 3,000 years ago. Since there was not much fire wood everything had to be cooked quickly over one fireplace. To do so the ingredients were cut up small – which leads us to the next utensil, the cleaver. Foodstuffs were chopped on kitchen utensil number three, a hard wooden chopping board. You would then stir everything with a spatula – already the last item on our list of Asian cooking utensils.

These utensils are so simple that they will never cease to fascinate. Their owners are surprisingly particular about their prized possessions, no matter whether you are dealing with a farmer's wife or an accomplished chef. Be careful and refuse any invitation to have a go at cutting the food yourself. These apparently harmless looking cleavers are so sharp that clumsy Western fingers just get in the way too easily.

We would now like to get down to the more serious stuff. Asian cuisine is thought through to perfection and despite their apparent simplicity the kitchen utensils do not lag behind.

Let us start with the wok, a very large pan with a convex base which can replace all other cooking pots. You can do just about anything with it: cook, simmer, fry, steam and even deep fry. Since Asian cuisine has taken a foothold in the West you can buy woks in all shapes and sizes and in a variety of materials. But none of them compare to the simple old and sturdy iron wok with a robust wooden handle. Our grandmothers would always have used a cast iron frying pan – a fact that is not easily comprehensible in the modern day, high-tech kitchen. But cast iron dissipates heat very evenly and some of the iron is even taken up by the food, adding a further healthy dimension.

When buying a wok you should always check its balance before handing over the cash. Woks with two handles are – perhaps surprisingly – less easy to work with than those with just the one long handle. Also, it is only worth getting a wok if you really are going to use it regularly. Should you only want to use it once in a while a large, deep frying pan will do just fine.

The spatula for stirring or ladling is a shovel like instrument with a long handle made out of wood or plastic. A skimmer or a wooden spatula will also do the trick. Chopping boards are a must in every kitchen. Round hardwood boards or a proper butcher's block are ideal (a butcher's block is not cheap but worth every penny because it will last for the whole of your life).

The cleaver is a real multi-tasker once you have mastered it. You can use it to cut, pare, beat, finely chop, peel, crush, mince and just about anything else that you might do in the kitchen. However, one thing you should not do – start chopping away. This will ruin your cleaver immediately. A well cared for hatchet will last just as long as your chopping boards.

We would now like to tell you all you need to know about the different ingredients and their preparation. However, one more word about the recipes. We took special care to choose only ingredients that are readily available in the UK. The ease with which you might come across them depends on whether you live in a large city or out in the country, down South or up North etc. etc... It might not always be possible to get hold of every single item at all times. In such cases you should follow the Asian rule and see the recipe as a mere suggestion that can be changed according to taste. We hope you will enjoy using your imagination and relish the results! By the way, Asian chefs improvise and experiment throughout their lives.

Asian cooking is about the preservation of colour, structure, aroma and taste of its ingredients. The individual items have to not only match perfectly but also be balanced to a tee. Such preparations often take more time than the actual cooking process. Cutting the ingredients in small bits is an excellent means of reducing cooking times. Special tastes are achieved by marinating. If some ingredients take longer to cook one simply blanches or pre-cooks them so that everything can be thrown into the pan together. Sometimes herbs or spices are fried first in order to flavour the oil for the next ingredients. Dried items are soaked. Take care not to pour away the water but use it later to add flavouring.

## COOKING METHODS

As a rule Asians ingest little raw food. Exceptions are fresh fruit or some Japanese specialities. Everything is somehow prepared, even if it only takes a few seconds rather than hours.

### Deep Frying

is the preferred way of cooking crispy samosas or pastry with juicy fillings.

### Simmering

is well known in the West. It means cooking on a very low temperature. This is ideal for large pieces of meat. If the lid has a tight fit your meat will cook evenly. Should you have an earthenware pot you will be spared having to add water or some other liquid as the meat cooks in its own juices.

### Roasting or Grilling

is reminiscent of our barbecue. Most of the time you put marinated pieces of meat on a skewer to be roasted over a charcoal grill. Ideal with spicy sauces.

Steaming is possible either with a normal wok and a little steamer made out of bamboo or a normal steaming set. Both methods supply the saturated heat required for successful steaming.

Stir frying is probably the most famous and popular way of cooking in Asia. You simply pour a little oil into the wok and add the ingredients. Stirring constantly on a high flame this way of cooking is very quick and nutritious while flavour remain intact.

Red-cooking means cooking meat, fish, poultry or vegetables in a mixture made of soy sauce, water and/or stock. The dishes are reddish brown in colour and taste slightly sweet while having a tart quality at the same time.

**Beverages**

What comes to mind if you think about Asian beverages? Tea, rice wine and beer? Yes, beer. This seemingly European or Western drink is also well known and extremely popular in Asia. Especially China, Japan, Korea, Hong Kong, Singapore and Taiwan possess national breweries which make excellent beer. And none of it goes to waste. Beer, unlike rice wine, however, is not an Asian invention. The first breweries were set up by Germans in China some 100 years ago. This shows how well foreign cultures are integrated into Asian life and used to complement or improve the regional cuisine.

Asian liqueurs, fermented juices and spirits should be available in well-stocked Asian shops or good restaurants: Umeshu, a Japanese plum liqueur and the Chinese Mao-tai, also known as "white lightning". The latter is a spirit made out of corn. You will only realise its full potential when you try to stand up! The plum liqueur is served on the rocks which is quite uncommon for an Asian drink. Spirits only fully develop their flavour when stored at room temperature or sometimes you even heat them up like rice wine. Having an ice cold drink before or during eating is an occurrence that is often frowned upon. It was introduced by Europeans and has the side effect of being bad for the stomach. But what makes it even worse is that you will not be able to taste your food properly any more because your taste buds have quite literally been put on ice.

Apart from tea, coffee is also a drink of choice in some countries. Water and fruit juices are ideal for quenching your thirst although one should always revert to bottled water to be on the safe side.

## CULINARY VOCABULARY

**Abalone**

also called ear shell, is an edible marine snail which has firm and tasty meat. Similar to turtles, the abalone's "great taste" is something they could do without. These days abalones are a protected species and it is illegal to catch them.

**Bamboo Sprouts**

are the young edible shoots of a certain kind of bamboo plant. They have a delicate nutty flavour and are a firm favourite in the Asian cuisine as a warm or cold vegetable side dish. You will normally encounter the tinned variety, although some specialist food stores may stock them fresh.

**Bonito flakes**

or ground bonito form the basis of every Japanese fish stock. The product is gained from dried sea fish, mainly tuna, and is available in specialist food shops.

**Chopsticks**

are Asian cutlery. Only those countries that have not experienced a great Chinese influence such as Thailand, Indonesia, Malaysia or the Philippines do not use them. Instead people eat with spoons, every now and then with a fork and spoon or quite simply with their fingers. Chopsticks are not the same wherever you go. Japanese sticks are shorter and have a sharper point than their Chinese counterparts. But notwithstanding their appearance, the effect remains the same. You concentrate on your food, eat slowly, enjoy the dish and digest properly. They are easier to eat with than you might think. The following picture shows how to hold them.

**Coconut Milk**

is not the juice from the inside the coconut but the liquid gained from its pulp. You can make it yourself by finely grating the coconut and pouring the same volume of hot water over it. Leave to soak a little while before squeezing everything through a kitchen towel. You could also use desiccated coconut or choose the simple alternative of buying tinned unsweetened coconut milk.

**Hoisin Sauce**

is the second most famous sauce after soy sauce. Again, it is used extensively especially in Chinese cooking. Its main ingredients are soy beans which are processed following a variety of traditional recipes to give different flavours.

**Kombu**

is the name the Japanese have given dried seaweed used, among others, for aromatic sushi rolls.

**Lychees**

have a fresh and aromatic flavour with just a hint of roses and nutmeg. Should you be lucky enough to come across them fresh at the local greengrocers or the supermarket do not hesitate but go and buy some. They taste much better than the over-sweetened tinned variety.

**Mirim**

is a slightly sweetened rice wine used mainly in Japanese cooking. If you find it impossible to get hold of you can always use dry sherry instead.

**Monosodium Glutamate**

is a crystalline flavour enhancer used extensively in Chinese cooking. It improves the flavour of the ingredients and softens the meat. However, because it is thought to cause some food allergies doctors nowadays recommend not to use it.

**Nori**

is what the Japanese call the "edible paper" made from seaweed. The very thin dark-green sheets should be roasted in a frying pan without any oil or butter so that they can fully develop their aroma.

**Oyster Sauce**

is a thick, brown sauce for seasoning. It is quite salty and should therefore be used sparingly.

**Sake**

is the world famous Japanese rice wine.

**Sambal Oelek**

is a devilishly hot paste made with a lot of

red chillies. Those who have been to an Indonesian restaurant will have more or less fond memories!

**Sesame Oil**
is an extremely aromatic oil. The light version is made from untreated grain while its darker counterpart has roasted grain. It is mainly used for seasoning.

**Shiitake Mushrooms**
are specially grown mushrooms from Japan that can even tempt the ardent fan of wood mushrooms. They have a great aroma, there is little waste, you can use them dried or frozen and they are entirely free of harmful substances.

**Shoots and Sprouts**
are aromatic, fresh, healthy and easy to grow. They have always been a firm favourite of the well-balanced and nutritional Asian cuisine. You will find the right grains in every good health food shop. The table below provides an overview.

**Snow Peas**
are very small, light green pods containing sweet tasting peas. They are easily grown in a vegetable garden but you have to take care to harvest them in time. If you leave them for too long they will lose their delicate aroma so that you will not want to eat them at all.

**Soy Sauce**
the one sauce no Asian cook could ever do without. Soy sauce is available in many different flavours. There are two main kinds – light and dark soy sauce. The light sauce is relatively mild in flavour and used to season dishes. Dark soy sauce is stronger, thicker and quite salty. More money does not always get you the better product, but in the case of soy sauce this is really the case. A good sauce does cost more because the fermentation of the soy beans needs time (similar to that of champagne).

**Sprouts and Shoots**

| Sort | Soaking Time (hrs) | Germination Time | Notes, Taste |
|---|---|---|---|
| Alfalfa | 4 to 6 | 5 | Especially rich in vitamins, a little bitter |
| Mostard | 12 | 6 to 12 | Stimulates digestion, heals the digestive tract, hot but mild |
| Sesame | 4 | 2 | Difficult to germinate, neutral |
| Millet | 8 | 3 | Good for the skin, rich in proteins and fluoride, sweet |
| Radish | 4 | 2 | Sharp and hot |
| Mung Beans | 12 | 5 | Easy to grow, good yield, nutty, does not get bitter when left too long |
| Chickpea | 12 | 3 | Rich in proteins, bitter when left too long, mealy, mild |
| Pea | 12 | 3 | Rich in proteins, very sweet |
| Yellow soy bean | 12 | 3 | Rich in proteins, juicy, neutral |

**Tamarind**
is mainly used as a seasoning in Indian cooking. The flavour is reminiscent of unripe plums.

**Tofu**
or bean curd, is a very nourishing vegetarian ingredient made from cooked soy beans. Tofu is rich in digestible proteins (approx. 1/2 oz/13 g to every 3 oz/100g), vitamins and minerals. Even better, it contains very little cholesterol. You can cook it in any number of ways. Ever since Asian cooking has become a firm favourite in Europe you can get hold of tofu in a variety of flavours ranging from natural (neutral in taste) right down to the well seasoned, smoked or marinated varieties.

**Wasabi**
is a green Japanese horseradish. Unlike its white counterpart it is hardly ever used fresh but can only be bought as a ground powder or paste.

**Water Chestnuts**
are the dark-brown, bulbous fruit of a particular water plant. Apart from the fact that you have to peel them before cooking they have nothing in common with nuts. The ones you will come across are usually tinned. It is possible to use bamboo shoots instead.

**Wood Ear Mushrooms**
or wood ear fungi are used mainly dried and are a firm favourite in every Asian kitchen. You have to soak them thoroughly before cooking. Should you not be able to get any you can use oyster mushrooms instead.

# SOUPS – A POT-POURRI OF FAR EASTERN DELICACIES

In Asia, even the most ordinary soup is regarded as something special. The different tastes of the ingredients have to be combined skilfully and harmonically. An Asian saying states that even a soup can reflect inner equilibrium.

# HOT CHICKPEA STEW

**Serves 4**

**10 oz (300 g) potatoes**

**1 onion**

**1 clove of garlic**

**1 tbsp oil for frying**

**7 oz (200 g) tinned chickpeas**

**1/2 tsp curcuma**

**1 tsp garam masala (Indian spice mixture containing cardamom pods, cinnamon, cumin, coriander seeds, cloves, mace, fennel seeds, black peppercorns)**

**pepper, salt**

**2 pints (1 l) chicken stock**

Preparation time: 15 minutes
Cooking time: 25 minutes
Energy per serving: approx. 1269 kJ/302 cal

1 Peel and dice the potatoes.

2 Also peel and dice the onions and the clove of garlic.

3 Heat the oil in a largish pan and brown the onions and garlic.

4 Drain the chickpeas using a colander. Transfer them to the onions and garlic. Add the potatoes.

5 Stir in the spices and fry everything for approximately 3 minutes, stirring continuously.

6 Pour in the chicken stock and leave to simmer on a low flame for another 15 minutes. Serve hot.

# SWEET AND SOUR WON-TON-SOUP

■ Serves 4

4 oz (125 g) flour

1/2 tsp lard

2 oz (60 g) cooked chicken breast

2 oz (60 g) sliced cold roast meat

salt

1/2 tsp monosodium glutamate

1 pinch pepper

1/2 tsp sesame oil

2 pints (1 l) chicken stock

1 piece fresh ginger (2 1/2 oz/70 g)

1 small leek

1 carrot

1 oz (30 g) tinned bamboo shoots cut into strips

2 tbsp sweet red bean paste

coriander leaves for decoration

Preparation time: 20 minutes
Cooking time: 20 minutes
Energy per serving: approx. 958 kJ/228 cal

1 Place the flour, lard and 2 tsp of water into a bowl and knead until you have a smooth dough. Sprinkle some flour on your working surface and roll out the dough until thin. Cut out 24 squares and make sure they are all the same size.

2 Finely dice the cooked chicken breast and the cold roast meat. Season with salt, monosodium glutamate, pepper and the sesame oil.

3 Spread the mixture onto one half of the dough squares. Wet the edges with water and place the other squares on top. Press down at the edges to make sure the won-tons are properly sealed. Transfer into simmering, slightly salted water and leave to cook for approximately 2 to 3 minutes. Remove, drain and place onto soup plates or into bowls.

4 Pour the chicken stock into a pot and bring to the boil.

5 Peel the fresh ginger and cut into thick slices. Add to the soup.

6 Wash or peel and finely slice the leek and the carrot. Add to the soup and continue to cook for approximately 4 to 5 minutes.

7 Drain the bamboo shoots using a colander and add to the soup together with the red bean paste.

8 Season the soup again with salt, pepper and monosodium glutamate if necessary. Transfer into soup plates/bowls and decorate with the coriander leaves. Serve.

# Soto

**Serves 4**

**1 beef bone containing bone marrow**

**7 oz (200 g) shin of beef**

**1 leek**

**4 slices fresh ginger (1/2 inch/1 cm each)**

**1 1/2 tbsp salt**

**2 tbsp ready-made roast onions**

**1 bunch chives**

Preparation time: 15 minutes
Cooking time: 1 1/2 hours
Energy per serving: approx. 380 kJ/90 cal

1 Wash the bone and the meat under the running cold tap.

2 Clean, wash and roughly slice the leek. Transfer the leek, ginger and meat into a large pot. Pour in 3 pints (1 1/2 litres) of water and sprinkle in the salt.

3 Bring to the boil. Skim the soup and leave to simmer on a medium heat for approximately 1 1/2 hours.

4 Sieve the soup and finely slice the meat and the slices of ginger. Put them back into the soup.

5 Sprinkle the roast onions into the soup. Transfer the soto into soup plates or bowls.

6 Wash and dry the chives using a salad spinner. Finely slice the chives, sprinkle over the soup and serve.

# THAI LEMON SOUP

1 Peel the king prawns and cut in half lengthwise. Remove the black intestines.

2 Cut the lemon grass into thin strips. Peel and finely dice the onions and the clove of garlic.

3 Halve, deseed and finely chop the chillies.

4 Pour the coconut milk into a pot, add 13 fl oz (400 ml) of water, the lemon grass, onions, garlic and the chillies and bring everything to the boil.

5 Add the king prawns and continue to simmer for approximately 3 minutes.

6 Season the soup with the brown sugar, juice of half a lemon and the fish sauce. Finely chop the lemon balm. Transfer the soup into soup plates and decorate with the lemon balm. Serve hot.

**Serves 4**

**8 king prawns**

**2 lemon grass stalks**

**2 onions**

**1 clove of garlic**

**2 chillies**

**10 fl oz (300 ml) coconut milk**

**1 tsp brown sugar**

**1/2 lemon**

**3 tbsp fish sauce**

**2 stalks lemon balm**

Preparation time: 15 minutes
Cooking time: 20 minutes
Energy per serving: approx. 548 kJ/ 130 cal

# CHINESE CABBAGE SOUP

**Serves 4**

**1 onion**

**1 clove of garlic**

**2 tbsp oil**

**salt**

**1 pint (500 ml) chicken stock**

**1 Chinese cabbage**

**1/2 pint (250 ml) coconut milk**

**1 bunch fresh coriander**

Preparation time: 15 minutes
Cooking time: 20 minutes
Energy per serving: approx. 409 kJ/97 cal

1 Peel and finely dice the onion and the clove of garlic.

2 Heat the oil in a pot and sauté the onion and garlic.

3 Pour in the chicken stock, add the salt and bring everything to the boil.

4 Remove the outermost leaves and halve the Chinese cabbage. Cut out the stalk and finely slice the cabbage.

5 Add the cabbage strips to the soup and leave to simmer for approximately 10 minutes. Pour in the coconut milk and bring to the boil once more, stirring continuously.

6 Wash and dry the fresh coriander using a salad spinner. Pluck the leaves off and sprinkle over the soup. Serve hot.

# Ebi Non Suimono (Fish Soup)

1 Wash the seaweed well and place in a pot. Add 1 1/2 pints (750 ml) of cold water and bring to the boil. Remove the seaweed.

2 Add the fish flakes to the simmering stock and leave to steep for some 2 minutes (the stock must not boil). Sift the fish soup and season with salt and the soy sauce.

3 Cut the fish fillet into strips, place in a bowl and cover with the sake. Leave to steep for a little while.

4 Clean and finely chop the spring onions. Peel and cut the carrots into fine strips.

5 Add the vegetables to the soup and leave to simmer for some 4 minutes.

6 Transfer the fish together with the sake to the soup and continue to simmer for some 3 minutes.

7 Transfer the soup into soup plates, decorate with the watercress and serve.

**Serves 4**

**1 piece dried seaweed**

**4 oz (125 g) dried fish flakes**

**2 tsp salt**

**1 tsp soy sauce**

**7 oz (200 g) fillet of ocean perch**

**2 tbsp sake**

**4 spring onions**

**3 carrots**

**watercress for decoration**

Preparation time: 10 minutes
Cooking time: 20 minutes
Energy per serving: approx. 520 kJ/124 cal

# NOODLE SOUP WITH PRAWN BALLS

■ **Serves 4**

**4 oz (125 g) peeled prawns**

**1 oz (30 g) lard**

**1 egg white**

**1 pinch salt**

**1 pinch monosodium glutamate**

**2 tsp ground ginger**

**1 tbsp cornflour**

**12 dried shiitake mushrooms**

**1 small tin bamboo shoots, sliced**

**3 pints (1 1/2 l) chicken stock**

**7 oz (200 g) Chinese egg noodles**

Preparation time: 30 minutes
Cooking time: 30 minutes
Energy per serving: approx. 1667 kJ/ 397 cal

1 Pass the peeled prawns and the lard through a mincer. Use a fine setting.

2 Mix together the prawn purée, egg white, salt, monosodium glutamate, the ground ginger and the cornflour until you have a smooth mousse. Work the mixture into little balls. Cook in simmering, slightly salted water for approximately 2 minutes.

3 Place the shiitake mushrooms into a bowl and cover with boiling water. Leave for approx. 30 minutes. Afterwards remove the stem by twisting it until it comes off and slice the mushrooms.

4 Drain the bamboo shoots using a sieve.

5 Pour the chicken stock into a saucepan and bring to the boil. Add the egg noodles and the mushrooms and cook until done.

6 Add the bamboo shoots and the prawn balls. Reheat and serve.

# Meatballs

Mix together 8 oz (250 g) minced beef, 1 egg white, 1 tsp ground ginger, 1 tsp sake, pepper, 1 tsp soy sauce and 1 tsp cornflour until you have a smooth dough. Work the mixture into balls which you cook in simmering, slightly salted water for approximately 10 minutes. Add to the noodle soup and decorate with watercress before serving.

**Serves 4**
Preparation time: 30 minutes
Cooking time: 30 minutes
Energy per serving: approx. 1597 kJ/ 380 cal

# Vegetable-Tofu Balls

Finely chop 8 oz (250 g) mixed vegetables (white cabbage, carrots, beans, onions, chillies) and 3 1/2 oz (100 g) tofu. Mix everything together. Add 1 tbsp tomato purée, 1 tsp ground ginger, 1 tbsp cornflour and 1 egg white and mix until you have a smooth dough. Work into little balls. Cook in simmering, slightly salted water and serve in the noodle soup.

**Serves 4**
Preparation time: 30 minutes
Cooking time: 30 minutes
Energy per serving: approx. 1452 kJ/ 345 cal

# KOREAN ONION SOUP

**Serves 4**
**8 oz (250 g) beef**
**1 clove of garlic**
**4 tbsp soy sauce**
**1 tbsp sesame seeds**
**pepper**
**1 tsp peanut oil**
**5 onions**
**1 bunch chives**

Preparation time: 20 minutes
Cooking time: 45 minutes
Energy per serving: approx. 639 kJ/152 cal

1 Wash the beef and dab it dry. Cut into diamond shaped slices.

2 Peel and finely dice the clove of garlic.

3 Mix together the soy sauce, sesame seeds, garlic, pepper and the meat.

4 Heat the oil in a pan and brown the meat on a high flame on all sides.

5 Pour in 3 pints (1 1/2 l) of water and leave the meat to simmer on a low heat for approximately 35 minutes.

6 Peel and cut the onions into rings. 15 minutes before the meat is done add the rings to the soup and cook until soft.

7 Wash and dry the chives using a salad spinner. Finely chop the chives and sprinkle over the soup. Serve hot.

## TIP

You could give the soup an extra spicy touch by adding only 2/3 of the onion rings to the soup and frying the other 1/3 until crisp. Leave to dry on a kitchen towel to absorb any excess fat and place on preheated soup plates. Add the soup and serve straight away.

# HOT LENTIL SOUP

**Serves 4**

**8 oz (250 g) red lentils**

**salt**

**1/2 tsp curcuma**

**4 oz (125 g) potatoes**

**7 oz (200 g) small onions**

**1 red pepper**

**1 chilli pepper**

**1 piece fresh ginger (1 inch/2 cm)**

**1 tomato**

**1 tin mango slices 4 oz (125 g)**

**1 tbsp oil**

**pepper**

**1 tbsp curry powder**

**1 tsp garam masala**

Preparation time: 20 minutes
Cooking time: 45 minutes
Energy per serving: approx. 1282 kJ/ 304 cal

1 Wash the lentils and cook in 2 pints (1 l) of slightly salted water for approximately 30 minutes. Add the curcuma and leave to cool.

2 Peel and dice the potatoes. Cook in slightly salted water for approximately 15 minutes.

3 Peel and halve the onions. Clean, halve, deseed and cut the pepper into fine strips. Clean, wash, halve, deseed and cut the chilli pepper into thin strips.

4 Peel and dice the fresh ginger. Skin, deseed and dice the tomato.

5 Purée the contents of the tinned mango (including the liquid) and the lentils (including their liquid) in a blender.

6 Heat the oil in a pan and sauté the onions, pepper, chilli and ginger.

7 Add the lentil and mango purée and bring everything to the boil.

8 Now add the potatoes and tomato, season with the spices until hot and serve.

# DUCK SOUP WITH WATERCRESS

**Serves 4**

**13 oz (400 g) breast of duck**

**4 slices fresh ginger (1/2 inch/1 cm each)**

**2 oz (60 g) parma ham**

**8 oz (250 g) watercress**

**2 tbsp sake**

**2 tsp soy sauce**

**1 tsp sugar**

Preparation time: 15 minutes
Cooking time: 2 1/2 hours
Energy per serving: approx. 1314 kJ/ 313 cal

1 Pour 3 pints (1 1/2 l) of water into a saucepan, add the breast of duck and the ginger. Cut the ham into cubes and transfer into the same pot.

2 Bring everything to the boil. Skim off the froth every now and then and leave to simmer on a low heat for approximately 1 1/2 to 2 hours.

3 Wash and pluck the leaves of the watercress.

4 Cut the breast of duck and into strips. Put it back into the soup and add the watercress. Leave to simmer for 15 minutes.

5 Season with the sake, soy sauce and the sugar and serve hot.

# Curry Soup

1 Wash, dry and finely slice the chicken breast.

2 Heat the oil in a pan and brown the meat on all sides together with the ground cashew nuts.

3 Sprinkle in the curry, add the stock. Bring to the boil and turn down the heat.

4 Peel and dice the potatoes. Wash and finely chop the broad beans. Peel and dice the carrots.

5 Transfer the vegetables to the soup and add the bay leaf. Leave to simmer on a low heat for approximately 20 minutes.

6 Add the coconut milk, stirring continuously. Heat the soup again and season with salt.

7 Transfer the soup into soup plates or bowls, sprinkle over the roast onions and serve hot.

**Serves 4**

**4 oz (125 g) chicken breasts**

**2 tbsp oil**

**1 tsp ground cashew nuts**

**1 pinch curry powder**

**1 pint (500 ml) chicken stock**

**3 oz (100 g) potatoes**

**5 oz (150 g) broad beans**

**5 oz (150 g) carrots**

**1 bay leaf**

**1/2 pint (250 ml) coconut milk**

**salt**

**1 tbsp ready-made roast onions**

Preparation time: 20 minutes
Cooking time: 35 minutes
Energy per serving: approx. 750 kJ/178 cal

# Starters and Side Dishes – Spicy, Fragrant, Crunchy Titbits

Asian cuisine has a bewildering choice of imaginative titbits and side dishes. They are as numerous and varied as the people in Asia which makes it difficult to give a representative sample of recipes.

# Bengali Chapati with Mint Chutney

**Serves 4**
**8 oz (250 g) potatoes**
**salt**
**1 onion**
**12 oz (375 g) flour**
**3 tbsp oil**
**butter for frying**

**For the chutney:**
**1 bunch mint**
**1 chilli pepper**
**2 onions**
**1 clove of garlic**
**juice from 1/2 lemon**
**salt**
**paprika**
**1 pinch ground ginger**
**1 pinch garam masala**
**sprigs of mint for decoration**

Preparation time: 30 minutes
Cooking time: 50 minutes
Energy per serving: approx. 1889 kJ/ 452 cal

1 Wash and peel the potatoes. Cook in slightly salted water for 20 minutes.

2 Peel and finely dice the onions.

3 Mix together the flour, salt, oil and onions. Mash the potatoes and stir into the mixture until you have a smooth dough. Divide into 4 equal portions. Roll out the dough to make 4 chapatis with a diameter of 6 inches/15 centimetres each.

4 Melt the butter in a pan and cook the chapatis for 5 minutes each.

5 To make the mint chutney, wash the mint and dry using a salad spinner. Transfer into a blender.

6 Clean, halve and deseed the chilli pepper and add to the blender.

7 Peel the onion and the clove of garlic, chop coarsely and place in the blender.

8 Add the lemon juice and purée everything. Season with salt, paprika, ground ginger and garam masala. Arrange the chapatis on plates and spread on the chutney. Decorate with the sprigs of mint and serve.

# SWEET AND SOUR APPETIZERS

**Serves 4**

**12 scallops**

**1 spring onion**

**1 thick slice of fresh ginger (1/2 inch/ 1 cm thick)**

**salt**

**4 tbsp vinegar**

**2 tsp sugar**

**1 tbsp light soy sauce**

**1 tsp dark soy sauce**

**2 tbsp sesame oil**

**1 radish**

**1 tin bamboo shoots**

**2 thick carrots**

**slices of cucumber for decoration**

Preparation time: 15 minutes
Cooking time (excluding marinating time): 20 minutes
Energy per serving: approx. 640 kJ/152 cal

1 Wash the scallops.

2 Put enough water in a saucepan for the scallops to be covered. Add the spring onion, the fresh ginger and salt and bring to the boil. Add the scallops and continue to boil until the shells open.

3 Take the scallops out of the water and remove the mussel meat. Leave to cool and cut into slices.

4 Mix together the vinegar, sugar, the two different soy sauces and the sesame oil to make a marinade.

5 Peel the radish and cut into finger thick strips.

6 Drain the bamboo shoots using a colander and cut into finger thick strips.

7 Peel the carrots and cut into finger thick strips. Pour over 1/4 of the marinade and leave to steep.

8 Of the remaining marinade, pour a 1/4 each over the scallops, the radish and the bamboo shoots. Leave to steep.

9 Remove the appetizers from the marinade and arrange on a plate. Decorate with the cucumber slices and serve.

# FRIED RICE

**Serves 4**

**10 oz (300 g) rice**

**salt**

**4 eggs**

**3 tbsp rice wine**

**1 tbsp soy sauce**

**oil for frying**

**1 leek**

**7 oz (200 g) mixed minced meat**

Preparation time: 20 minutes
Cooking time: 35 minutes
Energy per serving: approx. 1297 kJ/ 309 cal

1 Cook the rice in enough slightly salted water for approximately 20 minutes.

2 Whisk the eggs and add the rice wine and 1 tsp of soy sauce.

3 Heat the oil in a frying pan, add the egg mixture and fry while stirring continuously. Remove when cooked and tear into small pieces.

4 Wash and cut the leek into rings. Heat some oil, sauté the leek for a short while before removing it again.

5 Heat some oil in the frying pan and brown the minced meat. Make sure the meat is well separated and does not clump together. Season with 1 tsp of soy sauce. Remove and put to one side.

6 Drain the rice, rinse under the running cold tap and leave to cool. Heat some oil and reheat the rice. Add the other ingredients and season with the rest of the soy sauce. Arrange on plates and serve.

# Coloured Noodle Salad

1 Cook the glass noodles in slightly salted boiling water for approximately 2 minutes. Drain, rinse under the running cold tap and leave to cool.

2 Wash the fillet of fish, cut into bite sized pieces and cook in slightly, salted simmering water for approximately 10 minutes. Remove and leave to cool.

3 Wash and slice the cucumber. Halve, deseed and dice the peppers.

4 Peel and finely chop the onions. Halve, deseed and finely chop the chillies.

5 Mix together the lemon juice, sugar and the fish sauce. Add the onions and chillies.

6 Wash and dry the lemon balm using a salad spinner. Then finely chop it and stir into the salad dressing.

7 Add the dressing to the salad ingredients and toss well. Arrange on plates and serve.

**Serves 4**

**2 1/2 oz (75 g) glass noodles**

**salt**

**3 1/2 oz (100 g) fillet of fish**

**1 cucumber**

**1 yellow pepper**

**1 red pepper**

**2 onions**

**2 red chillies**

**3 tbsp lemon juice**

**1 tbsp sugar**

**2 tbsp fish sauce**

**1 sprig lemon balm**

Preparation time: 10 minutes
Cooking time: 20 minutes
Energy per serving: approx. 738 kJ/175 cal

# SHRIMP SLICES

**Serves 4**

**8 oz (250 g) peeled, boiled shrimps**

**2 onions**

**2 cloves of garlic**

**salt**

**pepper**

**1 tsp ground ginger**

**1 tsp lemon juice**

**2 eggs**

**5 slices white bread without the crust**

**oil for frying**

**4 big oranges**

Preparation time: 15 minutes
Cooking time: 20 minutes
Energy per serving: approx. 1371 kJ/ 326 cal

1 Wash and dry the shrimps using a salad spinner. Then chop them finely.

2 Peel and dice the onions and cloves of garlic and add to the shrimps.

3 Season everything with salt, pepper, ground ginger and the lemon juice.

4 Add the eggs and mix until you have a smooth mixture. Spread on the slices of bread.

5 Cut the bread into bite sized pieces. Heat the oil in a frying pan and brown the pieces of bread with the mixture face down. Then turn the pieces over to brown the bread.

6 Peel the oranges and cut out the segments. Make a deep incision in the back of each segment but avoid cutting it in half.

7 Open up the segments and arrange on plates. Place the shrimp slices on top of the segments and serve.

# EGGS IN CHILLI SAUCE

1 Peel and finely dice the onions and cloves of garlic.

2 Halve, deseed and finely chop the chillies.

3 Heat the oil in a frying pan and sauté the onions, garlic and chillies.

4 Skin the tomatoes and remove the green flesh around the stalk. Then chop them coarsely. Add to the frying pan.

5 Pour in the chicken stock and coconut milk while stirring continuously. Bring everything to the boil. Leave to simmer on a low heat for approximately 15 minutes. Season with the sambal oelek and the sugar.

6 Peel the eggs and place in the sauce until hot. If you prefer it, you can also cut them in half.

7 Arrange the eggs and sauce on plates, decorate with the coriander leaves and serve.

**Serves 4**

**2 onions**

**2 cloves of garlic**

**3 red chilli peppers**

**2 tbsp sesame oil**

**3 tomatoes**

**1/2 pint (250 ml) chicken stock**

**1/2 pint (250 ml) coconut milk**

**1 tsp sambal oelek**

**1 tsp sugar**

**4 hard boiled eggs**

**coriander leaves for decoration**

Preparation time: 15 minutes
Cooking time: 30 minutes
Energy per serving: approx. 772 kJ/184 cal

# BEEF KEBABS WITH CHILLI AND PEANUT SAUCE

**Serves 4**

**1 lb (500 g) lean beef**
**2 onions**
**2 cloves of garlic**
**1 tbsp brown sugar**
**2 tbsp curry powder**
**1 pinch ground cumin**
**3 cloves**
**1 tbsp peanut butter**

**For the sauce:**
**2 chilli peppers**
**3 tbsp sesame oil**
**2 tsp peanut butter**
**1 tsp shrimp paste**
**2 tsp brown sugar**
**1 tbsp lemon juice**

Preparation time: 20 minutes
Cooking time: 40 minutes
Energy per serving: approx. 1294 kJ/ 308 cal

1 Wash, dry and cut the beef into strips.

2 Peel and dice the onions and the cloves of garlic. Mix together with the sugar, curry powder, ground cumin, cloves and the peanut butter. Add sufficient water to achieve a smooth mixture.

3 Cover the meat with the sauce and stick on skewers. Grill the meat until it is done and crisp and brown on all sides.

4 To make the sauce, halve, deseed and finely chop the chillies.

5 Heat the sesame oil in a frying pan and sauté the chillies together with the peanut butter, the shrimp paste and the sugar.

6 Add the lemon juice and simmer everything on a low heat for approximately 30 minutes. Serve as a sauce for the beef kebabs.

# ONION SAUCE

Finely dice 2 onions, 2 chillies and 1 clove of garlic. Transfer everything to a blender and add 1 tsp sugar, 1 tsp garam masala, 2 tbsp lemon juice and 2 tsp of water. Purée to a fine paste. Serve the sauce as an accompaniment to the beef kebabs.

**Serves 4**
Preparation time: 20 minutes
Cooking time: 20 minutes
Energy per serving: approx. 919 kJ/219 cal

# TOMATO SAUCE

Skin, deseed and finely chop 10 oz (300 g) of tomatoes. Mix together with 1 tsp shrimp paste and 2 tbsp finely chopped coriander leaves and leave to steep for approximately 2 hours. Serve the sauce as an accompaniment to the beef kebabs.

**Serves 4**
Preparation time: 20 minutes
Cooking time (excluding marinating time): 15 minutes
Energy per serving: approx. 959 kJ/228 cal

# INDONESIAN FRIED NOODLES

**Serves 4**

**2 pints (1 l) coconut milk**

**5 chilli peppers**

**1 tsp crab paste**

**1/2 tsp salt**

**2 tbsp desiccated coconut**

**2 tsp coriander seeds**

**1 bunch fresh coriander**

**10 oz (300 g) Asian egg noodles**

**peanut oil for frying**

Preparation time: 30 minutes
Cooking time: 30 minutes
Energy per serving: approx. 1584 kJ/ 377 cal

1 Simmer the coconut milk on a low flame for approximately 30 minutes. Stir from time to time.

2 Halve, deseed and finely chop the chillies.

3 Place the crab paste, chillies, salt, desiccated coconut and the coriander seeds into a mortar and grind it well with a pestle. Add the mixture to the coconut milk.

4 Wash the fresh coriander and dry using a salad spinner. Pluck off the leaves and add them to the sauce.

5 Cook the noodles in sufficient slightly salted water following the instructions on the packet. Drain and leave to dry a little.

6 Heat the oil in a frying pan and fry the noodles. Add the sauce and bring everything to the boil.

7 Transfer the noodles onto plates and serve.

## TIP

You always have to carefully deseed chilli peppers because it is the seeds that really make them hot – the same goes for all other capsicums. If you have sensitive skin make sure you wear gloves before handling the red hot little devils.

# TEMPURA

1 Clean and cut the shiitake mushrooms into bite sized pieces.

2 Wash, dry and cut the ocean perch into bite sized pieces. Clean the peeled prawns and put aside.

3 Wash and dry the aubergine and cut into slices about 1/2 inch/1 cm thick. Peel the radish and cut into bite sized pieces.

4 Coat the vegetables and fish pieces with flour.

5 Mix together the egg yolks, flour and 1/4 pint (125 ml) of ice cold water to make the batter. Cover the vegetable and fish pieces with the batter by dipping them into it. Then fry them in hot fat until golden brown and crispy.

6 In the meantime, mix together the rice wine and the soy sauce. Peel and finely dice the ginger. Halve, deseed and finely chop the chilli. Add the ginger, salt and chilli pepper to the sauce.

7 Arrange the fried tempura on plates and serve with the sauce.

**Serves 4**

**4 shiitake mushrooms**

**13 oz (400 g) fillet of ocean perch**

**4 peeled prawns**

**1 aubergine**

**1 radish**

**flour for coating**

**3 egg yolks**

**3 1/2 oz (100 g) flour**

**oil for frying**

**3 tbsp rice wine**

**6 tbsp soy sauce**

**1 piece fresh ginger (1 inch/2 cm)**

**1 chilli pepper**

**1 pinch salt**

Preparation time: 20 minutes
Cooking time: 20 minutes
Energy per serving: approx. 1454 kJ/ 346 cal

# Chinese Cabbage Wraps

**Serves 4**

**1 lb (500 g) seafish fillet**

**salt**

**8 oz (250 g) cooked rice**

**3 dried chillies**

**1 tsp dried lemon grass**

**1 tsp black peppercorns**

**1 tsp pimento berries**

**8 Chinese cabbage leaves**

**8 thin strips of leek to tie together the Chinese cabbage leaves**

**ready made Asian noodles with chilli and shrimp flavour as a side dish**

Preparation time: 15 minutes
Cooking time: 20 minutes
Energy per serving: approx. 700 kJ/166 cal (excluding the side dish)

1 Wash the fillet of fish and leave to cook in slightly salted, barely simmering water for approximately 10 minutes.

2 Transfer the fillet into a blender and purée.

3 Stir the blended fish into the cooked rice.

4 Place the dried chillies, peppercorns and pimento berries into a mortar and grind with a pestle. Use the mixture to season the rice.

5 Blanch the Chinese cabbage leaves in slightly salted boiling water for approximately 1 minute. Remove and leave to cool.

6 Spoon the seasoned rice and fish mixture onto the Chinese cabbage leaves. Take hold of a leaf's edges and pull upwards to form a pouch. Use a leek strip to secure the leaf. Repeat with the other seven leaves.

7 Place the wraps in slightly salted, barely simmering water until hot. Remove, arrange on plates and serve. Ideal with Asian noodles with chilli and shrimp flavour.

# Rice Croquettes with Lemon Dip

1 Mix together the minced meat, sesame seeds, pearl barley and the rice. Season the mixture with the soy sauce, salt and pepper.

2 Peel the clove of garlic, crush, add some salt and stir into the meat mixture. Also stir in the eggs.

3 Work the mixture into croquettes. Cover the croquettes with flour.

4 Heat the oil in a frying pan and fry the croquettes until cooked and brown on all sides.

5 Clean and chop the stalk of lemon grass. Grate the lemon rind and squeeze the juice out of the lemons.

6 Pour the lemon juice, fish sauce and rice wine vinegar into a saucepan. Add the lemon grass and grated lemon zest.

7 Peel and chop the ginger and add to the pan. Bring to the boil and take off the heat. Remove the lemon grass and purée in a blender.

8 Arrange the croquettes on plates and serve with the lemon dip.

**Serves 4**

**8 oz (250 g) mixed minced meat**

**2 tbsp sesame seeds**

**5 oz (150 g) cooked pearl barley**

**5 oz (150 g) cooked long grain rice**

**2 tbsp soy sauce**

**pepper**

**salt**

**1 clove of garlic**

**2 eggs**

**3 tbsp flour**

**oil for frying**

**1 stalk lemon grass**

**2 lemons**

**2 tbsp fish sauce**

**2 tbsp rice wine vinegar**

**1 piece fresh ginger (3/4 inch/2 cm)**

Preparation time: 15 minutes
Cooking time: 20 minutes
Energy per serving: approx. 2986 kJ/ 473 cal

# BAKED TOFU BALLS

**Serves 4**

**12 oz (350 g) tofu**
**1 egg**
**1 onion**
**2 cloves of garlic**
**1 bunch spring onions**
**1 tsp soy sauce**
**1 tsp five-spice powder**
**sesame oil for frying**

**For the sauce:**
**2 cloves of garlic**
**1 tbsp oil**
**2 tbsp peanut butter**
**2 tbsp soy sauce**
**1 pinch paprika**

Preparation time: 15 minutes
Cooking time: 25 minutes
Energy per serving: approx. 836 kJ/199 cal

1 Mash the tofu and stir in the egg.

2 Peel and finely dice the onion and the cloves of garlic.

3 Wash, dry and chop the spring onions. Mix everything together.

4 Season with the soy sauce and the powder and work into little balls.

5 Heat the oil in a frying pan and fry the tofu balls until they are golden brown.

6 To make the sauce, first peel and finely dice the cloves of garlic. Heat some oil in a frying pan and sauté the garlic. Add the peanut butter and pour in 1 pint (500 ml) of water. Bring everything to the boil and season with the soy sauce and the paprika.

7 Arrange the tofu balls on plates and serve with the sauce.

# OMELETTE "MANDARIN"

■ Serves 4

**10 dried wood ear mushrooms**

**1 bunch spring onions**

**1 piece fresh ginger (3/4 inches/2 cm)**

**7 oz (200 g) soy bean sprouts**

**1/4 pint (125 ml) chicken stock**

**1 tbsp oyster sauce**

**1 tbsp soy sauce**

**1 tsp sugar**

**1/2 tbsp cornflour**

**3 egg whites, 2 eggs**

**2 tbsp chicken stock**

**salt**

**oil for frying**

Preparation time: 15 minutes
Cooking time: 20 minutes
Energy per serving: approx. 499 kJ/119 cal

1 Pour boiling hot water over the wood ear mushrooms and leave to soak. When soft, cut into strips.

2 Wash and chop the spring onions. Peel and finely dice the fresh ginger. Clean and dry the soy bean sprouts using a salad spinner.

3 Mix together the oyster sauce, soy sauce, sugar and the cornflour. Put aside for the moment.

4 Whisk the egg whites until they are stiff. Put the eggs, 2 tbsp of chicken stock and the salt in a bowl and stir vigorously until it starts becoming foamy. Carefully fold the egg whites into the mixture.

5 Heat some oil in a frying pan and cook as many omelettes as possible.

6 Take a second frying pan, heat some oil and sauté the vegetables. Add the sauce and simmer on a low heat, stirring frequently. Make sure the vegetables remain firm to the bite.

7 Arrange the vegetables and omelettes on plates and serve.

# Sweetcorn Fritters with Cucumber Purée

**Serves 4**

- **2 onions**
- **2 cloves of garlic**
- **1 red pepper**
- **11 oz (340 g) tinned sweetcorn**
- **2 eggs**
- **1 tbsp flour**
- **1 pinch ground coriander**
- **1/2 tsp curcuma**
- **salt**
- **oil for frying**
- **1 cucumber**
- **1 bunch spring onions**
- **1 tbsp lemon juice**
- **1 tbsp rice wine vinegar**
- **1 tsp salt**
- **1 tsp sugar**
- **1 tsp soy sauce**

Preparation time: 15 minutes
Cooking time: 35 minutes
Energy per serving: approx. 861 kJ/205 cal

1 Peel and finely dice the onions and cloves of garlic.

2 Halve, deseed and finely dice the red pepper.

3 Drain the sweetcorn using a sieve and add to the onions, garlic and pepper.

4 Crack the eggs and mix with the flour. Add the spices and mix with the vegetables.

5 Heat the oil in a frying pan. Place small dollops of dough in it and cook the small fritters until done.

6 Peel and coarsely chop the cucumber.

7 Wash and coarsely chop the spring onions.

8 Mix together the lemon juice, rice wine vinegar, salt, sugar and the soy sauce. Pour everything into a pot and heat up.

9 Mix together the pieces of cucumber and the spring onions. Pour over the warm sauce and leave to steep for approximately 10 minutes.

10 Place everything into a blender, purée and serve together with the sweetcorn fritters.

# PHILIPPINE WRAPS

1 Wash the chicken breast and cook in barely simmering water until done. Leave to cool and cut into slices.

2 Peel and finely dice the onion and the cloves of garlic.

3 Dice the tofu.

4 Wash and finely slice the white cabbage.

5 Peel and dice the sweet potatoes.

6 Heat the oil in a frying pan and sauté the meat, garlic, onion, tofu, cabbage and the sweet potatoes.

7 Add the prawns and continue to cook for a short while.

8 Clean, slice and add the celery stalks to the frying pan.

9 Mix together the soy sauce and the sugar and add to the frying pan. Continue to simmer everything for approximately 10 minutes.

10 Mix together the flour, salt, egg and approximately 2 pints (1 l) of water until you have a smooth dough.

11 Heat some oil in a frying pan and cook thin omelettes until you have used up all the dough.

12 Spoon 2 tsp of the vegetable mixture onto each omelette, roll into a wrap and serve.

**Serves 4**

**1 chicken breast**

**2 cloves of garlic**

**1 onion**

**7 oz (200 g) tofu**

**10 oz (300 g) white cabbage**

**10 oz (300 g) sweet potatoes**

**1 tbsp peanut oil**

**7 oz (200 g) cooked and peeled prawns**

**5 oz (150 g) celery stalks**

**2 tbsp soy sauce**

**1 tbsp brown sugar**

**1 lb (500 g) flour**

**1 tbsp salt**

**1 egg**

**oil for frying**

Preparation time: 35 minutes
Cooking time: 45 minutes
Energy per serving: approx. 3058 kJ/ 728 cal

# Sushi with Trout Fillets

■ **Serves 4**

**2 thin fillets of trout (3 1/2 oz/100 g each)**

**2 tbsp salt**

**8 oz short grain rice**

**1 tbsp rice wine**

**2 tbsp rice wine vinegar**

**2 tsp sugar**

**6 tbsp rice vinegar**

**coriander leaves for decoration**

Preparation time (excluding marinating time): 25 minutes
Cooking time: 15 minutes
Energy per serving: approx. 544kJ/129 cal

1 Wash the trout fillets and rub all sides with salt. Put aside for 1 hour.

2 Rinse the rice under the running cold tap until the water runs clear.

3 Put the rice, approximately 1 pint (500 ml) of water, the rice wine and 1 tsp rice wine vinegar into a saucepan and bring to the boil. Leave to cook on a medium heat for approximately 15 minutes. Drain the rice, rinse under the cold running tap and stir in the rest of the rice wine vinegar and sugar. Leave to cool.

4 Wash the trout fillets thoroughly to remove the salt and place in a shallow bowl.

5 Pour the rice vinegar over the fish and leave to marinate for approximately 20 minutes.

6 Cut each trout fillet into 4 equal portions.

7 Divide the rice into 8 portions the same size as the trout fillets and press flat. Place the fish onto the rice platters. Decorate with the coriander leaves and serve.

# Sushi with Shrimps

1 Wash and blanch the spinach leaves in boiling water for approximately 2 minutes. Drain, lay on a flat surface and carefully dab until dry.

2 Rinse the rice under the running cold tap until the water runs clear. Put the rice, 1 pint (500 ml) of water and the sake into a pan and bring to the boil. Leave to cook on a medium heat for approximately 15 minutes.

3 Drain the rice, rinse under the cold running tap and stir in the rice vinegar, rice wine, salt and sugar. Leave to cool.

4 Cut the shrimps open along the back and remove the black intestines. Place in a shallow bowl.

5 Mix together the rice wine vinegar, Mirin and some sugar and pour the mixture over the shrimps. Leave to marinate for approximately 10 minutes.

6 Divide the rice into 16 portions and place onto the spinach leaves. Place a shrimp on each leaf and wrap tightly. Arrange the sushi on a plate and serve.

**Serves 4**

**16 medium sized spinach leaves**

**8 oz (225 g) short grain rice**

**1 tbsp sake**

**3 tbsp rice vinegar**

**1 pint (500 ml) rice wine**

**2 tsp sugar**

**1 tsp salt**

**16 cooked and peeled shrimps**

**3 tbsp rice wine vinegar**

**2 tbsp Mirin (sweet rice wine)**

**a little sugar**

Preparation time (excluding marinating time): 20 minutes
Cooking time: 20 minutes
Energy per serving: approx. 813 kJ/193 cal

# MEAT DISHES – CULINARY TREASURES OF THE SPECIAL KIND

In Asian cooking the correct preparation of the meat is much more important than expensive ingredients. Unlike in the West, the preparatory work takes up the lion's share of the total cooking time. The most important task is how to cut the meat properly, a process that takes place exclusively in the kitchen and never at the table or on the dinner plate.

# LAMB STEW

**Serves 4**

**2 lb (1 kg) lamb**

**1 onion**

**1 piece fresh ginger (3/4 inch/2 cm)**

**1 tsp garam masala**

**1 tsp salt**

**2 tbsp oil**

**8 oz (250 g) rice**

**1 pinch curcuma**

**4 cloves**

Preparation time: 15 minutes
Cooking time: 1 hour
Energy per serving: approx. 1874 kJ/ 446 cal

1 Wash the meat and dab dry with a kitchen towel. Cut into bite sized pieces.

2 Peel and coarsely chop the onion and the fresh ginger and place in a saucepan together with the meat, the garam masala, salt and sufficient water. Bring to the boil and simmer on a low flame for approximately 1 hour. Remove the meat, sift the stock using a fine meshed sieve and put the stock and the meat to one side.

3 Heat the oil in a frying pan and sauté the rice. Pour in 3/4 of the lamb stock and add the curcuma and cloves. Bring to the boil. Leave to simmer on a low flame for approximately 20 minutes or until all the liquid has evaporated, whichever takes longer.

4 Stir the meat into the rice, arrange on plates and serve.

# MEATBALLS IN RICE LEAVES

**Serves 4**

**1 lettuce**

**approx. 20 small rice leaves**

**2 oz (60 g) peanut butter**

**1 pinch dried and ground chillies**

**2 tbsp lime juice**

**6 tbsp oyster sauce**

**1/4 pint (125 ml) coconut milk**

**1 lb (500 g) mixed minced meat**

**1 bunch chives**

**2 cloves of garlic**

**1 spring onion**

**1 tsp finely chopped lemon grass**

**2 tbsp rice wine**

**1 egg**

**1 tbsp potato starch**

**1 tbsp sesame oil**

**salt, pepper**

**oil for frying**

Preparation time: 20 minutes
Cooking time: 20 minutes
Energy per serving: approx. 1948 kJ/ 464 cal

1 Pluck the lettuce. Wash and dry the leaves well using a salad spinner. Put to one side.

2 Soak the rice leaves in water.

3 Mix together the peanut butter, ground chillies, lime juice, oyster sauce and the coconut milk and put to one side.

4 Place the minced meat in a bowl.

5 Wash and dry the chives using a salad spinner. Chop finely and add to the meat. Make sure you keep a little for decoration.

6 Peel and finely chop the cloves of garlic and spring onion and add to the meat. Stir in the lemon grass, rice wine, the egg, potato starch and the sesame oil. Knead until you have a smooth dough and season with salt and pepper.

7 Work the mixture into little balls. Heat some oil in a frying pan and cook the meatballs until they are golden brown on all sides. Take out of the frying pan and place on a kitchen towel to remove any excess oil.

8 Wrap each meatball first in a lettuce leaf and then in a rice leaf. Arrange on plates and sprinkle with the leftover chives. Serve immediately with the sauce.

# Spicy Beef

**Serves 4**

**1 1/2 lb (750 g) beef**

**1 tin Chinese vegetables (net weight 8 oz/250 g)**

**3 tbsp peanut oil for frying**

**fresh ginger (3/4 inch/2 cm)**

**1 small clove of garlic**

**1/2 cup vegetable stock**

**6 tbsp white wine vinegar**

**2–3 tsp potato starch**

**4 tbsp tomato ketchup**

**salt**

**pepper**

Preparation time: 1 hour
Cooking time: 15 minutes
Energy per serving: approx. 1624 kJ/ 386 cal

1 Wrap the beef with cling film and place in the freezer for approximately 1 hour. That way you will be able to cut it very finely. Remove from the freezer and slice very thinly.

2 Drain the vegetables using a sieve and a bowl to preserve the liquid. Put both to one side.

3 Heat the oil in frying a pan until very hot. Add the meat and brown from all sides. Remove from the frying pan and put aside.

4 Place the Chinese vegetables into the frying pan and sauté. Take off the heat and put to one side.

5 Peel and finely dice the fresh ginger and the clove of garlic. Sauté in the frying pan and add the vegetable stock, white wine vinegar, potato starch and the ketchup. Bring to the boil and leave to simmer on a low flame for approximately 5–6 minutes. Season with salt and pepper.

6 Add the meat to the sauce and reheat. Serve immediately. Black rice which you steam in a covered bamboo basket over boiling water, makes an ideal accompaniment to this dish.

# Aubergines in Egg Latices

1 Wash the aubergines. Remove the green stalk and scrape out the flesh to within 1/2 to 3/4 inch (1 1/2 to 2 centimetres) of the skin. Finely chop the pulp.

2 Roast the cashew nuts in a frying pan without any oil or margarine. Peel and finely chop the clove of garlic.

3 Cut off the lower part of the lemon grass. Wash and chop finely. Wash and finely chop the spring onion.

4 Crack one egg and add to the meat. Also add the chopped aubergine pulp and mix until you have a smooth mixture. Season with the chilli sauce. Spoon the meat mix into the scooped out aubergines.

5 Heat the oil in a deep frying pan.

6 Mix together 2 oz (60 g) of the flour with a little water until you have a smooth dough-like mixture. First cover the aubergines with flour before dipping them into the mixture.

7 Deep-fry the aubergines in the hot oil for approximately 3 minutes. Remove and place on a kitchen towel to remove any excess oil.

8 For the egg latice whisk the rest of the eggs and fill into an icing bag with a very fine nozzle. Heat some oil in a non-stick frying pan. Squeeze the icing bag following a latice like pattern. Leave the egg to set and remove carefully. You will need 4 of these egg latices altogether.

9 Cut the aubergines into slices and arrange on the latices. Serve.

**Serves 4**

- **4 small aubergines**
- **2 oz (50 g) chopped cashew nuts**
- **1 clove of garlic**
- **3 stalks lemon grass**
- **1 spring onion**
- **4 eggs**
- **10 oz (300 g) minced beef**
- **chilli sauce**
- **oil for frying**
- **3 1/2 oz (100 g) flour**

Preparation time: 30 minutes
Cooking time: 20 minutes
Energy per serving: approx. 2073 kJ/ 493 cal

# PORK IN COCONUT SAUCE

**Serves 4**

**6 large wood ear mushrooms**

**1 lb (500 g) lean pork**

**1 tsp potato starch**

**1/2 red pepper**

**1/2 yellow pepper**

**2 tbsp sesame oil**

**3/4 pint (375 ml) coconut milk**

**2 tbsp oyster sauce**

**salt**

**pepper**

**sugar**

Preparation time: 20 minutes
Cooking time: 20 minutes
Energy per serving: approx. 1044 kJ/ 261 cal

1 Cover the large wood ear mushrooms with approximately 1 pint (500 ml) of boiling water and leave to soak for some 20 minutes. You can reuse the flavoured water at a later stage if you wish. It is perfect, for example, for thinning sauces that have become too thick.

2 Finely slice the pork and turn over in the potato starch.

3 Wash, deseed and cut the peppers into diamond shapes. Squeeze the wood ear mushrooms and cut into smaller pieces if necessary.

4 Heat the oil in a frying pan until very hot. Brown the strips of meat from both sides. Remove and put to one side.

5 Now place the peppers and the wood ear mushrooms into the frying pan and sauté.

6 Add the meat again and pour in the coconut milk. Season with the oyster sauce, salt, pepper and the sugar and leave to simmer on a low flame for a couple of minutes for the sauce to thicken. Arrange on plates and serve immediately.

# TERIYAKI STEAKS

1 Wash the steaks and dab dry with a kitchen towel. Place them in a shallow bowl.

2 Mix together 1 tsp sugar, the rice wine, soy sauce and the sesame oil and pour over the meat. Leave to marinate for approximately 30 minutes.

3 In the meantime, clean, peel and cut the carrot and the fresh ginger into small strips.

4 Mix together the vinegar, the rest of the sugar and 1 tsp of oil and pour over the vegetables. Leave to marinate for approximately 10 minutes.

5 Wash and dry the chives using a salad spinner. Chop finely. Roast the pumpkin seeds in a frying pan without any oil or margarine. Put both to one side.

6 Heat some oil in a frying pan until very hot. Remove the rump steaks from the marinade, leave to drain and fry on each side for approximately 2 to 3 minutes.

7 Remove the steaks and cut into bite sized pieces. Drain the vegetable strips and arrange together with the meat on plates. Wash the orange and tear off a long, thin strip of peel, making sure the end is still attached to the orange. Slice the fruit and use to decorate the main dish. Sprinkle with the chopped chives and roast pumpkin seeds. Serve immediately.

**Serves 4**

**4 rump steaks (5 oz/150 g each)**

**2 tsp sugar**

**1 tbsp rice wine**

**3 tbsp soy sauce**

**1 tbsp sesame oil**

**1 thick carrot**

**5 oz (150 g) radish**

**fresh ginger (3/4 inch/2 cm)**

**6 tbsp distilled vinegar**

**4 tbsp peanut oil**

**1/2 bunch chives**

**2 tbsp pumpkin seeds**

**1/2 orange for decoration**

Preparation time: 30 minutes
Cooking time: 15 minutes
Energy per serving: approx. 1708 kJ/ 406 cal

# FRIED LIVER CHINESE STYLE

**Serves 4**

**4 dried wood ear mushrooms**

**2 cloves of garlic**

**1 onion**

**3 spring onions**

**1 lb (450 g) veal or beef liver**

**oil for frying**

**3 tbsp light soy sauce**

**black pepper**

**2 tbsp hoisin sauce**

**1 tbsp cornflour**

Preparation time: 30 minutes
Cooking time: 25 minutes
Energy per serving: approx. 1688 kJ/ 402 cal

1 Cover the wood ear mushrooms with boiling water and leave to soak for 30 minutes. Slice after soaking.

2 Peel and finely dice the onions and cloves of garlic.

3 Wash and coarsely chop the spring onions.

4 Wash and dry the liver. Slice the liver.

5 Heat the oil and sauté onion and garlic.

6 Add the liver and brown on all sides.

7 Mix together the pepper, hoisin sauce and the potato starch and add the wood ear mushrooms. Pour the mixture into the frying pan, bring to the boil and leave to simmer on a low flame for approximately 15 minutes. Arrange on plates and serve.

# FRIED LIVER BALINESE STYLE

The preparation of this dish is similar to the Chinese version. In addition, however, you will need to add curcuma, ground chillies, 1 bay leaf and 1 tsp of chopped tomatoes to the sauce.

**Serves 4**
Preparation time: 30 minutes
Cooking time: 25 minutes
Energy per serving: approx. 1696 kJ/ 404 cal

# FRIED LIVER THAI STYLE

Heat some oil in a frying pan and add 1 lb (450 g) sliced liver, 1 peeled and diced clove of garlic, 1 peeled and diced onion, 1 finely chopped chilli pepper, 2 stalks of finely chopped lemon grass and chopped coriander leaves. Sprinkle with some cornflour and pour in 3 tbsp of water. Bring to the boil. Clean and peel 2 carrots and cut into small sticks and add to the liver. Leave to simmer on a low flame for approximately 15 minutes.

**Serves 4**
Preparation time: 30 minutes
Cooking time: 25 minutes
Energy per serving: approx. 1738 kJ/ 414 cal

# Great Mongolian Meat and Vegetable Stew

**Serves 4**

**1 lb (500 g) fillet of beef**

**1/2 pint (250 ml) soy sauce**

**2 tbsp rice wine**

**1 tsp sugar**

**2 onions**

**1 piece fresh ginger (2 inches/5 cm)**

**1 red pepper**

**1 aubergine**

**1/2 Chinese cabbage**

**3 1/2 oz (100 g) shiitake mushrooms**

**oil for frying**

**1 tsp cornflour**

Preparation time: 35 minutes
Cooking time: 20 minutes
Energy per serving: approx. 1264 kJ/ 301 cal

1 Wash and dry the fillet of beef. Cut into 1/2 inch/1 cm thick slices and place into a shallow bowl.

2 Mix together the soy sauce, rice wine and the sugar and pour over the meat. Leave to marinate for some 30 minutes.

3 In the meantime clean or peel the vegetable. Cut the onions into rings and slice the ginger, pepper, aubergine, shiitake mushrooms and the Chinese cabbage.

4 Remove the meat from the marinade and leave to dry.

5 Heat some oil in a frying pan and brown the meat on all sides. Fry until done. Remove and put to one side.

6 Now sauté each vegetable separately and put to one side. Keep warm.

7 Finally add all ingredients to the frying pan and reheat.

8 Mix together the rest of the marinade, stir in the cornflour and add the mixture to the frying pan. Bring to the boil, arrange on plates and serve.

# Beef Rolls

1 Slice the fillet of beef very thinly before gently beating it to tenderise the slices.

2 Mix together a little salt, sugar and the five-spice mixture with the oil until you have a smooth paste. Spread on the meat and leave to marinate for some 20 minutes.

3 Peel the thick carrots, quarter lengthwise and cook together with the cleaned English asparagus in boiling water for approximately 15 minutes.

4 Clean, deseed and finely chop the chilli pepper. Peel and finely dice the small carrot. Mix together the chilli, carrot, oyster sauce, 6 tsp of water and the lemon juice. Put aside to serve with the meat.

5 Place the boiled pieces of carrot and asparagus onto the meat and roll up to form longish tubes. Secure with a thread and dust with the potato starch.

6 Heat the oil in a frying pan and brown the rolls from all sides. Remove from the pan and place on a kitchen towel to drain off any excess oil. Cut into slices.

7 Pluck the leaves off the lettuce, wash and dry using a salad spinner and arrange on plates. Decoratively place the specially cut pieces of carrot around the edges of the plates. Arrange the meat rolls in the middle, garnish with the coriander leaves and serve immediately.

**Serves 4**

**13 oz (400 g) fillet of beef**

**salt, sugar**

**1 tsp five-spice powder**

**1 tbsp soy oil**

**2 thick carrots**

**8 oz (250 g) English asparagus**

**1 red chilli pepper**

**1 small carrot**

**6 tbsp oyster sauce**

**2 tbsp lemon juice**

**1 tbsp potato starch**

**oil for frying**

**frisée or iceberg lettuce, fancy shaped carrot pieces and coriander leaves for decoration**

Preparation time: 35 minutes
Cooking time: 20 minutes
Energy per serving: approx. 1107 kJ/ 265 cal

# MARINATED SPARE RIBS

■ **Serves 4**

**4 lb (2 kg) thin spare ribs**

**1 onion**

**4 cloves of garlic**

**1/2 pint (250 ml) rice wine**

**8 tbsp soy sauce**

**8 tbsp ketchup**

**5 tbsp honey**

**5 tbsp rice wine vinegar**

**2 tbsp oil**

**1 bay leaf**

**1 tsp ground cumin**

Preparation time (excluding marinating time): 15 minutes
Cooking time: 50 minutes
Energy per serving: approx. 1633 kJ/389 cal (excluding the side dish)

1 Wash and dry the ribs using a kitchen towel. Divide into portions.

2 Peel and dice the onion and cloves of garlic.

3 Mix together the rice wine, soy sauce, ketchup, honey, rice wine vinegar and the oil and stir in the bay leaf and the ground cumin.

4 Pour over the diced onion and garlic and add the ribs.

5 Leave to marinate for approximately 5 hours. Remove, dab dry with a kitchen towel and grill for some 50 minutes turning the ribs frequently. Serve with ready made Asian noodles kari curry flavour.

# ASIAN FRICASSEE

1 Peel and dice the onion and cloves of garlic.

2 Heat the oil in a frying pan and sauté the onion and garlic.

3 Wash, dry and cut the beef into slices. Add to the frying pan and brown from all sides.

4 Wash and skin the tomatoes. Remove the green flesh around the stalk and slice the tomatoes. Place in the frying pan. Pour in 1 1/2 pints (3/4 l) of water and stir well. Season with salt and pepper. Leave to simmer on a low flame for approximately 25 minutes.

5 Slice the veal liver. Peel and dice the potatoes. Add together with the liver to the meat.

6 Wash, halve, deseed and cut the red peppers into strips. Add to the frying pan and continue to cook for another 20 minutes. Serve hot.

**Serves 4**

**2 cloves of garlic**

**1 onion**

**2 tbsp oil**

**1 lb 4 oz (600 g) haunch of beef**

**2 tomatoes**

**salt**

**1 pinch of pepper**

**8 oz (250 g) veal liver**

**5 medium sized potatoes**

**2 red peppers**

Preparation time: 15 minutes
Cooking time: 45 minutes
Energy per serving: approx. 1896 kJ/ 451 cal

# BEEF CURRY

- **Serves 4**

**1 stalk lemon grass**

**2 cloves of garlic**

**1 onion**

**1 chilli pepper**

**2 tbsp sesame oil**

**1 tbsp ground ginger**

**1 tbsp curry powder**

**1/2 tsp ground cumin**

**1/2 tsp ground cardamom**

**1 tbsp freshly grated coconut**

**1 1/2 lb (800 g) beef**

**14 fl oz (400 ml) coconut milk**

**1/2 pint (1/4 l) beef stock**

**coriander leaves for decoration**

Preparation time: 20 minutes
Cooking time: 50 minutes
Energy per serving: approx. 1478 kJ/ 352 cal

1 Finely chop the lower half of the stalk of lemon grass.

2 Peel and dice the onion and cloves of garlic.

3 Wash, dry, halve, deseed and finely chop the chilli pepper. Heat the oil in a frying pan and sauté everything together.

4 Add the spices and the freshly grated coconut.

5 Wash and dry the meat using a kitchen towel. Cut into strips. Add to the frying pan and brown on all sides.

6 Pour in the coconut milk and the beef stock and leave to simmer on a low flame for approximately 40 minutes.

7 Arrange the beef curry on plates, decorate with the coriander leaves and serve.

# BEEFSTEAKS WITH TOMATO CHUTNEY

1 Peel and finely dice the onion, cloves of garlic and the fresh ginger. Mix together with the minced beef.

2 Add the egg and mix well. Work into rissoles.

3 Heat the oil in a frying pan and brown the rissoles from all sides until golden brown and done.

4 To make the chutney, skin and coarsely chop the tomatoes.

5 Wash, dry, halve, deseed and finely chop the chillies.

6 Peel and crush the cloves of garlic. Peel and finely chop the fresh ginger. Place in a saucepan together with the tomatoes, vinegar, sugar and salt and bring to the boil. Turn down the heat immediately.

7 Leave to simmer until the chutney achieves the desired consistency.

8 Arrange the rissoles on plates together with the cooled down tomato chutney and serve.

**Serves 4**

**1 onion**

**2 cloves of garlic**

**1 piece fresh ginger (1 1/4 inches/3 cm)**

**1 lb (500 g) minced beef**

**1 egg**

**1 pinch chilli powder**

**1 tsp ground cumin**

**1/2 tsp pink peppercorns**

**1/2 tsp ground coriander**

**1 pinch ground cinnamon**

**2 tbsp oil for frying**

**For the chutney:**

**1 lb (500 g) tomatoes**

**2 red chilli peppers**

**2 cloves of garlic**

**1 piece fresh ginger (3/4 inch/2 cm)**

**1/2 pint (250 ml) vinegar**

**7 oz (200 g) sugar**

**1 tsp salt**

Preparation time: 20 minutes
Cooking time: 1 hour
Energy per serving: approx. 1915 kJ/ 456 cal

# LEG OF LAMB IN RICE WINE

**Serves 4**

**1 leg of lamb**

**6 cloves of garlic**

**1 piece fresh ginger (1 1/4 inches/3 cm)**

**1 tsp ground cloves**

**1 pinch ground caraway seeds**

**1 pinch ground coriander**

**1 pinch ground star-anise**

**1 tsp pepper**

**1 leek**

**1 tbsp sesame oil**

**4 tbsp soy sauce**

**3 tbsp rice wine**

Preparation time: 25 minutes
Cooking time: 2 hours
Energy per serving: approx. 2086 kJ/ 496 cal

1 Wash and dry the leg of lamb using a kitchen towel.

2 Peel and crush the cloves of garlic.

3 Peel and finely chop the fresh ginger. Mix together with the garlic, ground cloves, ground caraway seeds, ground star-anise and the pepper.

4 Pour boiling water over the leg of lamb and leave for approximately 10 minutes. Drain and rub the spice mixture all over the leg of lamb.

5 Wash and slice the leek. Heat the oil in a saucepan, add the meat and the leeks, cover with a lid and leave to simmer on a low heat for approximately 30 minutes.

6 Pour in the soy sauce and the rice wine and continue to simmer for another 1 1/2 hours. Remove the leg of lamb, cut into slices and serve.

# COLD MEAT PLATTER WITH SALAD

1 Wash the meat and simmer in slightly salted water.

2 Remove the tongue of veal after 80 minutes, remove the skin and leave to cool.

3 Remove the shoulder of pork after 1 1/2 hours and leave to cool, too.

4 Remove the beef after 2 hours, drain and leave to cool. Slice the tongue, the pork and the beef and place on a plate.

5 Mix together the soy sauce, sugar and the vinegar and sprinkle over the meat.

6 For the salad, peel and cut the carrots into small sticks. Wash and finely slice the Chinese cabbage.

7 Clean the celery, remove the tough stringy bits and wash before slicing it.

8 Wash the soy bean sprouts and leave to drain well.

9 Mix all the vegetables together.

10 Mix together the vinegar, sugar, salt and the oil. Pour the salad dressing over the salad and toss well. Arrange on a plate and sprinkle over the pine kernels and sesame seeds. Serve together with the meat platter.

**Serves 4**

**1 veal tongue**

**1 1/2 lb (750 g) shoulder of pork**

**1 1/2 lb (750 g) brisket of beef**

**2 tsp salt**

**4 tbsp soy sauce**

**1 tbsp sugar**

**3 tbsp vinegar**

**For the salad:**

**4 carrots**

**1/2 Chinese cabbage**

**1 stalk celery**

**7 oz (200 g) soy bean sprouts**

**2 tbsp vinegar**

**2 tsp sugar**

**2 tsp salt**

**3 tbsp oil**

**1 tbsp chopped pine kernels**

**1 tbsp sesame seeds**

Preparation time: 10 minutes
Cooking time: 2 hours
Energy per serving: approx. 2365 kJ/ 563 cal

# Stir Fried Minced Meat with Rice Noodles

**Serves 4**

**2 cloves of garlic**

**2 onions**

**1 piece fresh ginger (3/4 inch/2 cm)**

**1 small tin water chestnuts (4 oz/ 125 g)**

**2 tbsp oil for frying**

**1 lb (500 g) mixed minced meat**

**4 tbsp soy sauce**

**1 tbsp cornflour**

**1 tsp sugar**

**1/2 tsp salt**

**8 oz (250 g) rice noodles**

**oil for deep frying**

Preparation time: 15 minutes
Cooking time: 20 minutes
Energy per serving: approx. 2681 kJ/ 638 cal

1 Peel and finely dice the cloves of garlic, onions and the fresh ginger.

2 Drain the water chestnuts using a colander and chop coarsely.

3 Heat the oil in a frying pan and sauté the chopped vegetables.

4 Add the minced meat and brown while stirring continuously.

5 Mix together the soy sauce, cornflour, sugar, salt and 1/4 pint (1/8 l) of water and pour into the frying pan. Leave to simmer on a low flame for approximately 5 minutes.

6 Cook the noodles following the instructions on the packet. Drain using a sieve, rinse under the running cold tap and leave to dry for a moment. Fry the four portions of noodles separately, arrange on plates together with the mixed meat and serve.

# FILLET OF PORK WITH PEAS AND BEANS

1 Wash, dry and slice the fillet of pork.

2 Peel the onions and cut into rings.

3 Heat the oil in a frying pan, sauté the onion rings and brown the meat.

4 Mix together the soy sauce, sugar and the rice wine and pour into the frying pan. Bring to the boil and leave to simmer on a medium flame for approximately 20 minutes.

5 Add the peas and beans.

6 Drain the bamboo shoots using a sieve and add to the meat.

7 Mix together the chicken stock and the monosodium glutamate and add to the frying pan. Bring to the boil once more, arrange on plates and serve.

**Serves 4**

**8 oz (250 g) fillet of pork**

**3 onions**

**2 tbsp oil for frying**

**4 tbsp soy sauce**

**2 tbsp sugar**

**3 tbsp rice wine**

**7 oz (200 g) broad beans, cooked**

**5 oz (150 g) cooked peas**

**1 tin bamboo shoots, sliced**

**2 tbsp chicken stock**

**1 tbsp cornflour**

**1 tsp monosodium glutamate**

Preparation time: 15 minutes
Cooking time: 35 minutes
Energy per serving: approx. 1207 kJ/ 287 cal

# MEATBALLS ON RICE

**Serves 4**

1 onion

2 cloves of garlic

1 lb (500 g) mixed minced meat

1 tsp soy sauce

1 pinch ground cumin

1 pinch ground coriander

1 pinch ground cardamom

black pepper

1 pinch monosodium glutamate

1 egg

2 tbsp cornflour

oil for frying

For the rice:

1 onion

2 cloves of garlic

2 tbsp ghee

1 pinch cinnamon

1 tbsp cardamom pods

2 cloves

1 tsp saffron

8 oz (250 g) rice

1 1/2 pints (750 ml) chicken stock

3 1/2 oz (100 g) raisins

2 oz (60 g) chopped almonds

Preparation time: 15 minutes
Cooking time: 45 minutes
Energy per serving: approx. 2800 kJ/ 666 cal

1 Peel and finely dice the onion and the cloves of garlic.

2 Mix together the minced meat, onions, garlic, spices and the egg. Work the meat into little balls and turn them over in the cornflour. Heat some oil in a frying pan and brown the meatballs from all sides. Remove and keep warm.

3 For the rice peel and finely dice the onion and cloves of garlic. Heat the ghee in a frying pan and sauté until the onion and garlic are translucent. Add the spices.

4 Add the rice and stir. Pour in the chicken stock and leave to simmer on a low flame for approximately 20 minutes.

5 Stir the raisins and chopped almonds into the cooked rice and serve together with the meatballs.

# Meatballs on Rice Chinese Style

Fry 8 oz (250 g) rice in some oil and pour in 1 1/2 pints (750 ml) beef stock. Leave to simmer on a low flame for approximately 20 minutes. Stir in 1 small tin of bamboo shoots (sliced), 5 oz (150 g) soy bean sprouts and 3 1/2 oz (100g) sautéed leeks. Arrange the meatballs on the rice and serve.

**Serves 4**
Preparation time: 15 minutes
Cooking time: 45 minutes
Energy per serving: approx. 2240 kJ/ 533 cal

# Meatballs on Rice Malaysian Style

Fry 8 oz (250 g) rice in some oil and stir in 1 tbsp mixed spices (chilli powder, black pepper, ground coriander, ground aniseed, curcuma). Pour in 1 1/2 pints (750 ml) chicken stock and leave to simmer on a low flame for approximately 20 minutes. Arrange on plates, add the meatballs and serve.

**Serves 4**
Preparation time: 15 minutes
Cooking time: 45 minutes
Energy per serving: approx. 2138 kJ/ 509 cal

# PORK CUTLETS IN HOT BEAN SAUCE

**Serves 4**

**4 pork cutlets**
**2 tbsp soy sauce**
**2 tbsp rice wine**
**1 tsp sugar**
**1 clove of garlic**
**oil for frying**
**3 tbsp black bean paste**
**2 tsp cornflour**

Preparation time (excluding marinating time): 15 minutes
Cooking time: 25 minutes
Energy per serving: approx. 2005 kJ/ 477 cal

1 Wash the cutlets and dry using a kitchen towel. Cut into smaller pieces and leave a bone on each piece if at all possible.

2 Mix together the soy sauce, rice wine and the sugar. Peel and crush the clove of garlic and add to the sauce.

3 Pour over the pork cutlets and leave to marinate for approximately 30 minutes.

4 Remove the meat and drain. Put the marinade to one side.

5 Heat the oil in a frying pan and brown the meat on all sides.

6 Mix together the marinade, black bean paste, cornflour and 3 tsp of water and pour into the frying pan. Bring to the boil and leave to simmer for approximately 10 minutes. Arrange on plates and serve together with the sauce.

# STIR FRIED MEAT WITH EGG RICE

1 Cook the rice in sufficient slightly salted boiling water for approximately 20 minutes.

2 Wash, dry and cut the fillet of pork into strips.

3 Mix together the soy sauce, ground ginger and the rice wine and pour over the meat. Leave to marinate for approximately 30 minutes.

4 In the meantime wash and slice the leek.

5 Peel and finely dice the onions and cloves of garlic.

6 Whisk the eggs and stir in the soy sauce and the sambal oelek.

7 Remove the meat from the marinade and brown in very hot oil for 5 minutes.

8 Transfer the vegetables into the frying pan and sauté until done, stirring continuously. Remove and keep warm.

9 Pour the egg mixture into the frying pan and fry while stirring all the time.

10 Drain the rice, rinse under the running cold tap and leave to drain. Fry and add all the other ingredients. Reheat while stirring continuously. Arrange on plates and serve.

**Serves 4**

**8 oz (250 g) basmati rice**

**salt**

**1 lb (450 g) fillet of pork**

**1 tbsp soy sauce**

**1 tsp ground ginger**

**1 leek**

**2 cloves of garlic**

**2 onions**

**4 eggs**

**2 tsp light soy sauce**

**1/4 tsp sambal oelek**

**oil for frying**

Preparation time: 30 minutes
Cooking time: 35 minutes
Energy per serving: approx. 1589 kJ/ 378 cal

# Korean Hotpot

**Serves 4**

**5 oz (150 g) beef**
**6 tbsp soy sauce**
**3 tsp sugar**
**2 cloves of garlic**
**pepper**
**2 tbsp sesame seeds oil**
**5 oz (150 g) minced beef**
**2 tbsp pine kernels**
**5 eggs**
**flour to dip the meat in**
**4 small parsnips**
**salt**
**5 oz (150 g) liver of beef**
**5 shiitake mushrooms**

Preparation time: 1 hour
Cooking time: 30 minutes
Energy per serving: approx. 1860 kJ/ 443 cal

1 Wash and dry the beef using a kitchen towel. Cut into cubes.

2 Mix together the soy sauce and 1 tsp of sugar.

3 Peel and crush the cloves of garlic.

4 Mix together half a crushed clove of garlic, pepper and 2 tsp sesame seeds. Stir into the soy sauce and sugar mix.

5 Pour the marinade over half of the beef cubes and leave to marinate for approximately 30 minutes.

6 Remove the cubes and leave to drain. Heat some oil in a frying pan and brown from all sides. Remove and put to one side.

7 Mix together the rest of the beef cubes, 3 tbsp soy sauce, 2 tsp sugar, a crushed clove of garlic, 1 tsp sesame seeds and 1/2 tbsp oil. Leave to steep.

8 Mix together the minced beef, the rest of the soy sauce, half a crushed clove of garlic, the pepper, the rest of the sesame seeds and 1 tsp oil.

9 Work the meat mixture into small balls. Insert a pine kernel into each ball.

10 Whisk one of the eggs. Dip the meatballs into the flour and then into the whisked egg. Heat some oil in a frying pan and brown the meatballs on all sides until cooked. Put to one side.

11 Wash and peel the parsnips and cook in 2 pints (1 l) of slightly salted water. When ready, drain making sure you preserve the water. Slice the parsnips and put to one side.

12 Cook the liver in boiling water for approximately 3 minutes. Remove and cut into strips. Season with 1 pinch of salt. Dip into the flour and then into the whisked egg. Brown in the frying pan from all sides and put to one side.

13 Clean and slice the shiitake mushrooms and sauté in hot oil.

14 Separate 2 eggs. Whisk both the whites and the yolks separately. Fold the stiff egg whites into the yolks and cook omelettes from the egg mixture. Cut into strips and put to one side.

15 Boil the remaining eggs until hard. Peel and slice and put aside for decoration.

16 Line the hotpot with the sliced parsnips and place the raw diced beef on top. Add the sliced omelettes, shiitake mushrooms, liver strips and finally the cooked beef cubes.

17 Place the meatballs around the hotpot's flue. Finally decorate everything with the sliced hard boiled eggs.

18 Pour over the parsnip water and cook at the dinner table until done.

THE FINEST JAPANESE SAKE
LIGHT GEKKEIKAN

# Ragout of Lamb with Saffron

**Serves 4**

1 1/2 lb (750 g) lamb

1 onion

2 cloves of garlic

2 spring onions

1 piece fresh ginger (3/4 inch/2 cm)

oil for frying

1 tub of yoghurt (5 oz/150 g)

1 pinch ground cumin

1 pinch ground cloves

1 pinch ground cardamom

1/2 tsp cinnamon

1 tsp saffron

Preparation time: 20 minutes
Cooking time: 1 hour
Energy per serving: approx. 1286 kJ/ 306 cal

1 Wash and dry the lamb using a kitchen towel. Cut into cubes.

2 Peel and finely dice the onions and cloves of garlic.

3 Wash and coarsely chop the spring onions.

4 Peel and finely chop the fresh ginger.

5 Heat the oil in a frying pan and brown the lamb cubes from all sides.

6 Add the onions and garlic and sauté.

7 Add the spring onions and ginger and sauté. Pour in 1/2 pint (1/4 l) of water and leave to simmer on a medium flame for approximately 1 hour.

8 Mix together the yoghurt and the spices and add to the frying pan. Bring to the boil while stirring continuously. Arrange on plates and serve.

# Suckling Pig Casserole

**Serves 4**

**2 lb (1 kg) suckling pig meat**

**2 tbsp vinegar**

**2 tbsp brown sugar**

**4 tbsp soy sauce**

**2 tsp tamarind paste**

**1 bay leaf**

**1 tsp black pepper-corns**

**6 cloves of garlic**

**2 tbsp oil**

**1/2 pint (250 ml) rice wine**

Preparation time (excluding marinating time): 20 minutes
Cooking time: 75 minutes
Energy per serving: approx. 1467 kJ/ 349 cal

1 Wash and dry the meat using a kitchen towel. Cut into bite sized pieces.

2 Mix together the vinegar, sugar, soy sauce and the tamarind paste. Add the bay leaf and the black peppercorns.

3 Peel and crush the cloves of garlic and add to the marinade.

4 Pour the mixture over the meat and leave to marinate for approximately 1 hour.

5 Heat the oil in a frying pan. Remove the meat from the marinade and brown on all sides.

6 Add a little of the marinade and cook until the liquid is evaporated. Add the rice wine and 1/2 pint (250 ml) of water. Bring to the boil, cover with a tight fitting lid and leave to simmer on a low flame for approximately 1 hour.

7 Arrange the suckling pig casserole on plates and serve.

# CRISPY SADDLE OF BOAR

**Serves 4**

**1 saddle of boar (4–6 lb/1–2 kg)**

**1 tsp ground coriander**

**1 tsp ground black pepper**

**2 tbsp soy sauce**

**1 tbsp rice wine vinegar**

**1 tsp sugar**

**1 tsp cornflour**

**2 tbsp rice wine**

**chilli peppers and slices of cucumber for decoration**

Preparation time: 10 minutes
Cooking time: 70 minutes
Energy per serving: approx. 1283 kJ/ 305 cal

1 Wash the meat and dry using a kitchen towel. Rub thoroughly with the ground coriander and ground pepper.

2 Place the saddle of boar in an oven-proof dish and roast in the oven on gas mark 6 (400 °F or 200 °C) for approximately 1 hour.

3 Mix together the soy sauce, sugar and rice wine vinegar. Pour the mixture over the meat.

4 Leave the saddle of boar to roast for another hour. Baste every now and then with the sauce.

5 Remove the boar from the oven and keep warm.

6 Mix together the cornflour, rice wine and meat stock. Bring everything to the boil.

7 Arrange the saddle of boar on a plate, decorate with the chillies and the slices of cucumber and serve with the sauce.

# Spicy Kebabs with Sour Vegetables

1 Wash and cut the Chinese cabbage into broad strips. Cover with the salt and leave to sweat for approximately 30 minutes.

2 In the meantime peel and finely chop the onions and the ginger. Wash, halve, deseed and chop the chilli peppers. Peel the clove of garlic and crush together with some salt. Mix everything together.

3 Rinse the Chinese cabbage under the running cold tap and stir in the onion mixture. Place everything into an earthenware pot and cover with water. Cover with a tight fitting lid and leave to steep for one week.

4 Wash the beef, dry using a kitchen towel and cut into cubes.

5 Peel the white onions and the ginger and cut into 8 similar sized rings.

6 Alternatively thread the beef, the onion rings and the ginger onto skewers. Heat some oil in a frying pan and brown the kebabs from all sides.

7 Peel and finely dice the onion and the cloves of garlic. Wash, halve, deseed and dice the chilli peppers. Melt the butter in a frying pan and sauté the vegetables.

8 Add the curry powder and the tomato purée and stir well.

9 Pour in the beef stock and season with the lemon juice. Add the kebabs and leave to simmer on a low flame for approximately 10 minutes.

**Serves 4**

**1 Chinese cabbage**
**2 tbsp salt**
**3 onions**
**1 piece fresh ginger (1 1/4 inches/3 cm)**
**1 chilli pepper**
**1 clove of garlic**
**salt**

**For the kebabs:**

**1 lb (500 g) beef**
**8 small white onions**
**1 piece fresh ginger (3 inches/8 cm)**
**2 tbsp oil for frying**
**1 onion**
**2 cloves of garlic**
**3 chilli peppers**
**butter for frying**
**1 tbsp curry powder**
**1 tbsp tomato purée**
**4 tbsp beef stock**
**lemon juice**

Preparation time (excluding the sour vegetables): 20 minutes
Cooking time: 20 minutes
Energy per serving: approx. 1080 kJ/ 257 cal

# FISH AND SEAFOOD DISHES – FROM SIMPLE TO EXTRAVAGANT

Asian fish and seafood recipes count amongst the best in the world. This is because the manifold rivers, lakes and seas in and around the continent have contributed.

# Red-Cooked Squid

**Serves 4**

**2 tbsp rice wine vinegar**

**3 tbsp soy sauce**

**1/2 tsp sugar**

**1 tbsp peanut oil**

**1 lb (500 g) frozen squid rings**

**1 tbsp oil**

**chives for decoration**

Preparation time: 10 minutes
Cooking time: 15 minutes
Energy per serving: approx. 588 kJ/ 140 cal

1 Mix together the vinegar, soy sauce, sugar and the peanut oil.

2 Place the squid rings in a sieve and leave to defrost.

3 Heat the oil in a frying pan and brown the defrosted squid rings on all sides.

4 Pour the sauce over the squid rings and leave everything to simmer on a low flame for approximately 10 minutes.

5 Wash and dry the chives using a salad spinner. Chop them finely.

6 Arrange the squid on plates and sprinkle with the chives. Serve.

# BAKED HAKE WITH VEGETABLE YOGHURT

■ **Serves 4**

**2 lb (1 kg) fillet of hake**

**2 cloves of garlic**

**1 piece fresh ginger (3/4 inch/2 cm)**

**1/2 bunch fresh coriander**

**1 tsp chilli powder**

**1 pinch curcuma**

**oil for frying**

**2 tubs of yoghurt**

**salt**

**pepper**

**2 tomatoes**

**1/2 cucumber**

**2 onions**

**1 red pepper**

Preparation time: 20 minutes
Cooking time: 30 minutes
Energy per serving: approx. 1074 kJ/ 255 cal

1 Wash and dry the fillet of hake.

2 Peel and finely chop the cloves of garlic and the fresh ginger.

3 Wash the fresh coriander and dry using a salad spinner. Chop finely and mix together with the garlic, ginger and the spices.

4 Rub the mixture into the fillets. Heat some oil in a frying pan and brown the fillets on all sides. Remove and keep warm.

5 Whisk together the yoghurt, salt and pepper.

6 Skin, deseed and dice the tomatoes. Peel and cut the cucumber into small sticks. Peel and finely dice the onions. Wash, dry, halve, deseed and cut the pepper into strips.

7 Stir the vegetables into the yoghurt mixture and serve together with the hake fillets.

# Mussels and Fried Noodles

**Serves 4**

**7 oz (200 g) glass noodles**

**3 tbsp oil**

**7 oz (200 g) leeks**

**1 tbsp peanut oil**

**15 tinned water chestnuts**

**salt**

**sugar**

**1 tsp monosodium glutamate**

**1 pint (500 ml) chicken stock**

**1 small tin bamboo shoots (sliced)**

**1 tin mussels (13 oz/380 g net weight)**

**2 tbsp cornflour**

Preparation time: 15 minutes
Cooking time: 25 minutes
Energy per serving: approx. 1298 kJ/ 309 cal

1 Cook the glass noodles in boiling water following the instructions on the packet.

2 Drain, heat some oil in a frying pan and fry the cooked noodles. Put to one side and keep warm.

3 Wash and cut the leeks into strips.

4 Heat the peanut oil and sauté the leeks. Drain the water chestnuts using a colander and add to the frying pan. Add the spices and stir-fry for approximately 3 minutes.

5 Pour in the chicken stock and bring to the boil.

6 Now drain the bamboo shoots and the mussels and add to the frying pan.

7 Mix together the cornflour and 3 tbsp of water until smooth and add to the frying pan. Continue to simmer for approximately 3 minutes.

8 Arrange the mussels on plates, add the glass noodles and serve.

# FISH WITH RICE AND TOMATOES

1 Peel and finely dice the onion and the cloves of garlic. Wash and dry the fresh coriander using a salad spinner. Chop finely.

2 Heat the oil in a frying pan and sauté the onions, garlic and the coriander.

3 Add the salt, curcuma and the desiccated coconut and stir well. Pour in the lemon juice.

4 Skin, slice and add the tomatoes. Stir fry everything for 5 minutes.

5 Wash, dry and cut the ocean perch into bite sized pieces. Add to the frying pan, bring everything to the boil and simmer on a low flame for approximately 10 minutes.

6 Melt the butter in a second frying pan or a wok and fry the rice until translucent. Add 10 fl oz (400 ml) of hot water, bring to the boil, cover with a tight fitting lid and leave to cook on a medium heat for approximately 20 minutes.

7 Transfer the fish on top of the rice, cover again and cook for a further 10 minutes. Remove, arrange on plates and serve.

**Serves 4**

**3 cloves of garlic**

**1 onion**

**1/2 bunch of fresh coriander**

**3 tbsp oil**

**1 tsp salt**

**1 tsp curcuma**

**2 tsp desiccated coconut**

**1 tsp garam masala**

**2 tsp lemon juice**

**3 tomatoes**

**1 lb (500 g) fillet of ocean perch**

**1 tbsp butter**

**4 oz (125 g) rice**

Preparation time: 20 minutes
Cooking time: 50 minutes
Energy per serving: approx. 1235 kJ/ 294 cal

# TUNA KEBABS

**Serves 4**

**1 1/2 lb (750 g) tuna fillets**

**2 tbsp sweet rice wine**

**1 pinch salt**

**2 tbsp oyster sauce**

**1 egg yolk**

**1 tsp five-spice powder**

**1 tsp cornflour**

**1 tsp soy sauce**

Preparation time (excluding marinating time): 15 minutes
Preparation time: 20 minutes
Energy per serving: approx. 917 kJ/218 cal

1 Wash, dry and cut the tuna fillets into chunky cubes.

2 Mix together the rice wine, salt, oyster sauce, egg yolk and the five-spice powder.

3 Pour the sauce over the fish and leave to marinate for approximately 20 minutes.

4 Remove the tuna from the marinade and thread onto skewers. Place under the grill and brown on all sides until brown and cooked. Keep on basting with the marinade from time to time.

5 Remove the kebabs and arrange on plates. Mix together the cornflour and soy sauce and stir into the cooking juices. Serve as a sauce for the kebabs.

# BURMESE FISH BALLS

1 Wash, halve, deseed and coarsely chop the chilli pepper.

2 Clean and coarsely chop the fish.

3 Peel and quarter the onion.

4 Peel the fresh ginger and the cloves of garlic. Transfer to a blender. Add the chilli and the fish and give it one or two good pulses.

5 Add the lemon juice, salt, cornflour and the curcuma to the fish mixture and work into balls.

6 Heat 1 tbsp of oil in a frying pan and fry the fish balls until golden brown on all sides.

7 Heat the remaining oil in another frying pan and add the coconut milk. Stir continuously and heat until nearly boiling. Now add the fish balls and leave to simmer until cooked. Arrange on plates and serve.

**Serves 4**

**1 chilli pepper**

**2 lb (1 kg) fillet of any seafish**

**1 onion**

**3 cloves of garlic**

**1 piece fresh ginger (3/4 inch/2 cm)**

**2 tbsp lemon juice**

**salt**

**1 tbsp cornflour**

**1 pinch curcuma**

**2 tbsp oil**

**1/2 pint (250 ml) coconut milk**

Preparation time: 15 minutes
Cooking time: 25 minutes
Energy per serving: approx. 1020 kJ/ 243 cal

# KING PRAWNS WITH RICE

**Serves 4**

**8 king prawns**

**1 egg**

**4 tbsp flour**

**oil for frying**

**8 oz (250 g) rice**

**1/4 pint (125 ml) fish stock**

**3 tbsp soy sauce**

**1 tsp sugar**

**3 tbsp rice wine**

**1 pinch monosodium glutamate**

**parsley for decoration**

Preparation time: 10 minutes
Cooking time: 35 minutes
Energy per serving: approx. 1053 kJ/ 250 cal

1 Peel the king prawns, make an incision along the back and remove the black intestines.

2 Mix together the egg, 2 tbsp of water and the flour until you have a smooth batter. Heat some oil in a frying pan, dip the king prawns into the mixture and fry until golden brown and crispy. Remove, get rid off any excess oil and keep warm.

3 Cook the rice for approximately 20 minutes. Drain, rinse under the running cold tap and leave to dry off a little.

4 Transfer the fish stock, soy sauce, sugar, monosodium glutamate and the rice wine to a pan and bring to the boil. Add the rice, reheat and arrange everything on plates together with the king prawns. Garnish with the parsley and serve.

# KING PRAWNS WITH GLASS NOODLES

Prepare and cook 3 1/2 oz (100 g) glass or rice noodles following the instructions on the packet. Leave to drain. Wash and cut 1 leek and 5 soaked Asian mushrooms into strips. Heat some oil in a frying pan and sauté the vegetables. Add the noodles and give it a good stir. Mix together 2 tbsp ketchup, 2 tbsp soy sauce, 1 tbsp rice wine and 1 tsp cornflour and pour the sauce over the noodles. Bring to the boil and serve together with the king prawns.

**Serves 4**
Preparation time: 15 minutes
Cooking time: 15 minutes
Energy per serving: approx. 975 kJ/232 cal

# KING PRAWNS WITH CHINESE CABBAGE

Peel and finely chop 2 onions, 2 cloves of garlic, 1 oz (30 g) fresh ginger and 2 stalks of lemon grass. Heat some oil in a frying pan and sauté the vegetables. Pour in 13 fl oz (400 ml) coconut milk and 1/4 pint (125 ml) chicken stock and bring to boil. Leave to simmer until it has the consistency of a proper sauce. Cut the Chinese cabbage into finger thick slices and fry in a frying pan. Then pour in the sauce. Reheat everything and serve together with the king prawns.

**Serves 4**
Preparation time: 15 minutes
Cooking time: 15 minutes
Energy per serving: approx. 961 kJ/229 cal

# Fish Terrine with Rice Cakes

**Serves 4**

**1 1/2 lb (750 g) fillet of fish**

**1 tsp salt**

**1/2 pint (250 ml) lemon juice**

**5 onions**

**5 cloves of garlic**

**3 pimento berries**

**1 bunch fresh coriander**

**8 leaves white gelatine**

**2 cups rice**

**oil for the baking tray**

Preparation time: 30 minutes
Cooking time (excluding cooling time): 35 minutes
Energy per serving: approx. 1123 kJ/ 267 cal

1 Wash and finely chop the fillet of fish and transfer into a large bowl.

2 Stir the salt into 1/2 cup of water and add the lemon juice. Pour over the fish and leave to steep for approximately 15 minutes.

3 Peel and finely chop the onions and the cloves of garlic. Crush the pimento berries.

4 Wash and dry the fresh coriander using a salad spinner and chop finely.

5 Soak the gelatine in cold water. Squeeze the fish until dryish. Make sure you catch the excess lemon marinade.

6 Mix together the chopped fish, onions, garlic, pimento and the coriander.

7 Bring the marinade to the boil. Squeeze the gelatine to get rid of any water and dissolve in the hot liquid. Leave to cool.

8 Mix together the gelatine and the fish mixture. Rinse a terrine with cold water and pour the mixture into it. Place the terrine in the refrigerator and leave it to set.

9 In the meantime cook the rice on a medium flame for 15 minutes. Grease a baking tray and spread the rice out evenly. Place on the middle tray of the oven and bake at gas mark 4 (350 °F or 180 °C) until has taken on a little colour. Then increase the heat to gas mark 7 (450 °F or 225 °C) and bake for a further 10 minutes. Remove from the oven, cut into little cakes and leave to cool.

10 Arrange the rice cakes and the fish terrine on plates and serve.

# SCALLOPS FROM THE WOK

1 Cook the Chinese egg noodles in sufficient boiling water for 5 minutes. Drain using a colander and keep warm.

2 Heat the oil in a wok and sauté the crab meat. Season with the pepper.

3 Mix together the soy sauce, cornflour, 1/2 pint (250 ml) of water, sesame oil and the salt and add to the wok. Bring to the boil, stirring continuously.

4 Add the noodles and put everything to one side. Keep warm.

5 Wash and coarsely chop the spring onions. Peel and dice the fresh ginger. Wash, drain and – depending on their size – halve the scallops.

6 Heat the peanut oil in the wok until very hot and sauté the spring onions and the ginger.

7 Add the scallops and the sake and stir-fry for approximately 2 minutes.

8 Mix together the soy sauce, cornflour, 4 tbsp of water, salt and sugar and pour the sauce over the scallops. Cook for another minute, stirring continuously.

9 Arrange the noodles on plates, add the scallops and serve.

## TIP

The best way of cutting ginger is as follows: first peel the root using a proper peeler. Make sure you remove all the hard and woody bits. Now flatten it with a broad knife or a cleaver. Then finely slice it at a right angle. The trick is that flattening the ginger root has weakened the structure of the stringy fibre, causing it to fall into small bits once cut.

**Serves 4**

**8 oz (250 g) Chinese egg noodles**

**2 tbsp oil**

**3 1/2 oz (100 g) tinned crab meat**

**pepper**

**2 tbsp soy sauce**

**1 tbsp cornflour**

**1 tbsp sesame oil**

**salt**

**3 spring onions**

**1 piece fresh ginger (1 1/4 inches/3 cm)**

**1 lb (500 g) scallops**

**3 tbsp peanut oil**

**1 tbsp sake**

**For the sauce:**

**2 tbsp soy sauce**

**1 tsp cornflour, salt and sugar**

Preparation time: 15 minutes
Cooking time: 20 minutes
Energy per serving: approx. 2033 kJ/ 484 cal

# TERIYAKI SALMON

**Serves 4**

**4 salmon steaks (4 oz/125 g each)**

**1/4 pint (125 ml) soy sauce, 3 tbsp rice wine**

**2 tsp sugar 1 pinch monosodium glutamate**

**2 tbsp soy oil**

**radish for decoration**

**Asian noodles abalone flavour as accompaniment**

Preparation time (excluding marinating time): 10 minutes
Cooking time: 20 minutes
Energy per serving: approx. 1500 kJ/ 357 cal (excluding side dish)

1 Wash and dab the salmon steaks dry using a kitchen towel. Place in a shallow bowl.

2 Mix together the soy sauce, rice wine, sugar, monosodium glutamate and the soy oil and pour the marinade over the salmon steaks.

3 Leave the fish to marinate for approximately 30 minutes. Then place it under the grill and cook for about 10 minutes on each side. Do not forget to brush it with the marinade every now and then.

4 Arrange the salmon steaks on plates, decorate with the radish and serve. Ready-made Asian noodles, abalone flavour, make for an ideal accompaniment to this dish.

# PRAWN OMELETTE

1 Cover the dried wood ear mushrooms with boiling water and leave to soak.

2 Wash and drain the prawns.

3 Mix together the salt, the monosodium glutamate and the ginger wine and pour over the prawns. Leave to marinate for approximately 20 minutes.

4 Wash and chop the spring onions. Drain the wood ear mushrooms, squeeze and cut into strips.

5 Mix together the eggs, egg whites and the chicken stock and whisk until fluffy.

6 Heat the oil in a wok and sauté the spring onions and the wood ear mushrooms for approximately 2 minutes. Then push towards the edge of the wok.

7 Remove the prawns from the marinade and place in the wok. Stir well.

8 Pour in the egg mixture and leave to set over a medium flame. When the bottom side is brown turn the omelette and cook from the other side. Remove from the wok and keep warm.

9 Mix together the soy sauce, chicken stock, cornflour, sugar, salt and the monosodium glutamate and pour into the wok. Bring to the boil and serve as sauce together with the omelette.

**Serves 4**

**6 dried wood ear mushrooms**

**7 oz (200 g) peeled and cleaned prawns**

**1 pinch salt**

**1 pinch monosodium glutamate**

**1 tbsp ginger wine**

**3 spring onions**

**2 eggs, 4 egg whites**

**2 tbsp chicken stock**

**oil for frying**

**For the sauce:**

**3 tbsp soy sauce**

**4 tbsp chicken stock**

**1 tbsp cornflour**

**1 tsp sugar**

**1/2 tsp salt**

**1 pinch monosodium glutamate**

Preparation time (excluding marinating time): 20 minutes
Cooking time: 20 minutes
Energy per serving: approx. 857 kJ/204 cal

# EEL CURRY

**Serves 4**

**2 onions**

**4 cloves of garlic**

**2 chillies**

**2 tbsp oil**

**2 tbsp curry powder**

**2 tsp tomato purée**

**1 tsp curcuma**

**1 1/2 lb (750 g) fresh eel**

**lemon juice**

Preparation time: 20 minutes
Cooking time: 20 minutes
Energy per serving: approx. 2446 kJ/ 582 cal

1 Peel and finely dice the onions and the cloves of garlic.

2 Wash, halve, deseed and finely chop the chillies.

3 Heat the oil in a frying pan and sauté the onions, garlic and the chillies.

4 Add the curry powder and give it a good stir.

5 Add the tomato purée, curcuma and enough water to get the consistency of a thick sauce.

6 Skin the fresh eel, debone and cut into chunky pieces. Add to the wok and leave to simmer on a low flame until done.

7 Season with the curry powder and lemon juice, arrange on plates and serve.

# King Prawns and Tofu from the Wok

■ **Serves 4**

**10 oz (300 g) king prawns**

**10 oz (300 g) tofu**

**1 bunch spring onions**

**3 tbsp sesame oil**

**3 tbsp oyster sauce**

**2 tbsp soy sauce**

**2 tsp cornflour**

**1/2 tsp sugar**

Preparation time: 20 minutes
Cooking time: 20 minutes
Energy per serving: approx. 1509 kJ/ 359 cal

1 Peel the king prawns. Cut them along their back and get rid off the black intestines. Wash and drain well.

2 Cut the tofu into largish cubes.

3 Wash and coarsely chop the spring onions.

4 Heat the oil in a wok, add the king prawns, tofu and the spring onions and stir-fry for approximately 5 minutes.

5 Mix together the oyster sauce, soy sauce, cornflour, sugar and 3 tbsp of water.

6 Pour the sauce into the wok and cook until enough liquid has evaporated to give you a thick sauce. Arrange everything on plates and serve.

# MACKEREL CASSEROLE

**Serves 4**

**1 lb (500 g) fresh fillets of mackerel**

**1 leek**

**2 shallots**

**1 clove of garlic**

**7 oz (200 g) radish**

**7 oz (200 g) soy been sprouts**

**1 tbsp sugar**

**4 tbsp soy sauce**

**1 tsp coarsely ground black pepper**

**1/2 tsp pickled ginger**

**1 tsp ground pimento berries**

**1 tsp sesame seeds**

Preparation time: 15 minutes
Cooking time: 20 minutes
Energy per serving: approx. 1221 kJ/ 290 cal

1 Wash, dry and coarsely dice the fillets of mackerel and transfer to an oven-proof dish.

2 Clean and slice the leek. Peel and dice the shallots and the clove of garlic.

3 Peel and coarsely slice the radish. Wash and dry the soy bean sprouts using a salad spinner. Sprinkle the vegetables over the fish in the oven-proof dish.

4 Mix together the sugar, soy sauce, pepper, pickled ginger, ground pimento and the sesame seeds and pour over the fish and the vegetables.

5 Place the oven-proof dish on the middle shelf in the oven and bake at gas mark 4 (350 °F or 180 °C) for approximately 20 minutes. Remove from the oven, arrange on plates and serve.

# Fried Sea Bream with Honey Sauce

1 Wash the sea bream, dry with a kitchen towel and season with salt and pepper. Sprinkle with the rice wine and leave to steep for a while.

2 Whisk the egg. Dip the breams in the whisked egg and then turn them over in the cornflour.

3 Heat the oil in a frying pan and brown the breams on all sides. Remove from the frying pan, place on a kitchen towel to drain off any excess oil and keep warm.

4 Peel and finely dice the ginger. Clean, wash, halve, deseed and finely chop the chillies. Wash and cut the spring onions into thin rings. Clean, halve, deseed and finely slice the pepper.

5 Heat the peanut oil in a frying pan and sauté the vegetables. Mix together the vinegar, honey, soy sauce and the cornflour and pour into the frying pan. Bring everything to the boil, arrange together with the breams on plates and serve.

**Serves 4**

**4 small gutted and cleaned sea breams**

**salt**

**pepper**

**2 tbsp rice wine**

**1 egg**

**2 tbsp cornflour**

**oil for frying**

**1 piece fresh ginger (3/4 inch/2 cm)**

**2 chillies**

**3 spring onions**

**1 green pepper**

**2 tbsp peanut oil**

**3 tbsp vinegar**

**2 tbsp honey**

**3 tbsp soy sauce**

**1 tbsp cornflour**

Preparation time: 15 minutes
Cooking time: 20 minutes
Energy per serving: approx. 1809 kJ/ 430 cal

# FISH FILLETS WITH GINGER

**Serves 4**

**6 shiitake mushrooms**

**3 spring onions**

**1 piece fresh ginger (1 1/2 inches/4 cm)**

**2 tbsp peanut oil**

**3 tbsp sugar**

**3 tbsp rice wine vinegar**

**1 tbsp soy sauce**

**1 tbsp cornflour**

**4 haddock or cod fillets (8 oz/250 g each)**

**8 oz (250 g) flour**

**1 tsp salt**

**1 tbsp sesame oil**

**oil for frying**

**parsley for decoration**

Preparation time: 20 minutes
Cooking time: 25 minutes
Energy per serving: approx. 2251 kJ/ 536 cal

1 Clean and slice the shiitake mushrooms.

2 Wash and coarsely chop the spring onions.

3 Peel and finely slice the fresh ginger.

4 Heat the oil in a frying pan and sauté the vegetables.

5 Mix together the sugar, vinegar, soy sauce, cornflour and 7 fl oz (200 ml) of water and pour into the frying pan. Bring everything to the boil and cook while stirring continuously until the sauce has thickened.

6 Wash and dry the fillets of fish.

7 Mix together the flour, salt and the oil. Add enough water to achieve a thick dough.

8 Dip the fillets of fish in the batter and fry in hot oil until crispy and brown. Arrange on plates, add the ginger sauce, decorate with the parsley and serve.

# SALMON TROUT IN SPICY BEAN SAUCE

1 Descale, degut and wash the fish thoroughly.

2 Place the fish on a large enough piece of aluminium foil. Fold up the edges in such a way that it resembles a baking tray.

3 Season the fish with salt and pepper. Mix the bean paste with a little water and brush on the fish.

4 Peel and dice the cloves of garlic. Wash, halve, deseed and dice the chilli pepper. Peel and finely slice the fresh ginger and sprinkle everything over the fish.

5 Pour 1/2 pint (250 ml) of water over the fish and place the aluminium foil into an oven-proof dish. Pour 3/4 inch (2 cm) worth of boiling water into the oven-proof dish and place on the middle shelf of the oven. Bake at gas mark 6 (400 °F or 200 °C) for approximately 30 minutes.

6 Remove the fish and keep warm.

7 Pour the liquid into a saucepan and bring to the boil. Mix together the soy sauce, monosodium glutamate, sugar and the cornflour and add to the sauce. Bring everything to the boil. Arrange the fish on a plate, pour over the sauce and decorate with the spring onions. Serve.

**Serves 4**

**1 salmon trout**

**salt**

**pepper**

**1 tbsp bean paste**

**3 cloves of garlic**

**1 chilli pepper**

**1 piece fresh ginger (3/4 inch/2 cm)**

**1 tbsp soy sauce**

**1 pinch monosodium glutamate**

**1 tsp sugar**

**1 tbsp cornflour**

**spring onions for decoration**

Preparation time: 15 minutes
Cooking time: 40 minutes
Energy per serving: approx. 908 kJ/ 216 cal

# CARP CHINESE STYLE

**Serves 4**

**3 dried shiitake mushrooms**

**1 gutted and cleaned carp**

**1 tbsp soy sauce**

**2 tbsp rice wine**

**1 tsp sugar**

**salt**

**3 tbsp sesame oil**

**2 oz (50 g) ginger**

**2 spring onions**

**1 red chilli pepper**

**1 Chinese cabbage**

**For the sauce:**

**4 tbsp oyster sauce**

**1 tbsp soy sauce**

**1 tbsp ginger wine**

**1 tsp cornflour**

Preparation time: 20 minutes
Cooking time: 45 minutes
Energy per serving: approx. 1522 kJ/ 362 cal

1 Cover the shiitake mushrooms with boiling water and leave to soak for approximately 20 minutes.

2 Wash the carp and make crosswise incisions on both sides.

3 Mix together the rice wine, sugar, salt and the oil and brush all over the fish.

4 Place the carp onto the steamer inset in a fish casserole.

5 Peel and slice the fresh ginger. Wash and cut the spring onions into thickish rings. Wash, halve, deseed and finely dice the chilli pepper. Clean and rip the Chinese cabbage into smallish pieces. Drain the shiitake mushrooms and squeeze well. Remove the stalks and cut into strips.

6 Place the vegetables around and onto the fish. Pour boiling water into the casserole, cover and steam the carp on a medium flame for approximately 40 minutes.

7 Mix together the oyster sauce, soy sauce, ginger wine and the cornflour. Pour into a pan and bring to the boil. Arrange the carp on a platter, pour over the sauce and serve.

# CARP INDONESIAN STYLE

Make crosswise incisions as indicated in the recipe opposite. Heat some oil in a large frying pan or a wok and fry the carp. Add 7 oz (200 g) mixed vegetables (carrots, potatoes, beans), 3 tbsp chopped water chestnuts and 1 tbsp curry powder and give everything a good stir. Pour in 1/2 pint (250 ml) coconut milk and cook until the carp is done.

**Serves 4**
Preparation time: 20 minutes
Cooking time: 30 minutes
Energy per serving: approx. 1189 kJ/ 283 cal

# CARP INDIAN STYLE

Make crosswise incisions as indicated in the recipe opposite. Place on the steamer inset of a fish casserole and pour over some coconut milk. Place 1 diced mango, 1 bunch fresh coriander, 2 finely chopped chillies and onion rings from 2 onions around the fish. Cook as described opposite, arrange on a platter and serve.

**Serves 4**
Preparation time: 15 minutes
Cooking time: 45 minutes
Energy per serving: approx. 1303 kJ/ 310 cal

# BRAISED FILLET OF PLAICE

**Serves 4**

**4 fillets of plaice**

**2 tbsp lemon juice**

**3 1/2 oz (100 g) carrots**

**1 onion,**
**4 fresh shiitake mushrooms**

**salt, pepper, monosodium glutamate**

**2 tbsp soy sauce**

**4 tbsp sake**

**12 ginkgo nuts**

**tomatoes for decoration**

Preparation time: 20 minutes
Cooking time: 25 minutes
Energy per serving: approx. 668 kJ/159 cal

1 Wash the fillets of plaice, sprinkle over the lemon juice and leave to steep.

2 Peel and cut the carrots into fine strips. Peel and dice the onion.

3 Clean and cut the fresh shiitake mushrooms into thin strips.

4 Spread out 4 sufficiently large sheets of aluminium foil and place the fillets of plaice on top. Sprinkle over the vegetables.

5 Fold up the edges of the aluminium foil and sprinkle the fillets with the spices. Then pour over the soy sauce and the sake.

6 Place the ginkgo nuts on top and close the aluminium foil packets.

7 Place the packets on the middle shelf in the oven and bake at gas mark 4 (350 °F or 180 °C) for approximately 20 minutes. Remove, arrange on plates, decorate with the tomatoes and serve.

# Spicy King Prawn Kebabs

**Serves 4**

**8 oz (250 g) ground peanuts**

**1 tbsp rice wine vinegar**

**1 tsp lemon juice**

**2 tsp chilli powder**

**2 tbsp sugar**

**1 tsp soy sauce**

**1 tbsp hoisin sauce**

**1 lb (500 g) king prawns**

**For the sauce:**

**4 tbsp soy sauce**

**2 tbsp sake**

**1 tbsp fish sauce**

**1 tbsp tomato ketchup**

Preparation time: 20 minutes
Cooking time: 15 minutes
Energy per serving: approx. 1645 kJ/ 391 cal

1 Roast the ground peanuts in a frying pan without any oil or margarine. Remove and mix together with the rice wine vinegar, lemon juice, chilli, sugar, soy sauce and the hoisin sauce. Put the marinade to one side.

2 Wash and peel the king prawns. Leave the tails intact. Cut the prawns along the back and take out the black intestines. Use the incision made when you degutted the prawns to fold the meat inside out.

3 Brush the marinade on the inside and thread the prawns on skewers. Grill from all sides. Keep on brushing the marinade onto the prawns while grilling.

4 Mix together the soy sauce, sake, fish sauce and the ketchup. Arrange the king prawn kebabs on plates and serve with the sauce as a dip.

## Tip

You can either use white (strong flavoured) or red (mild flavoured) rice wine vinegar. Alternatively, white or red wine vinegar or fruit vinegar will do as well.

# POULTRY DISHES – TENDER AND DELICATE

Poultry is very high up on the Asian cook's agenda. Everyone has their own favourite recipe and will leave no stone unturned to find opportunities to try this, that or the other new version. Creative cooking is the motto. Let's get started!

# SPICED CANTONESE CHICKEN

**Serves 4**

**oil for frying**
**5 oz (150 g) walnuts**
**4 chicken breasts**
**2 tbsp soy sauce**
**3 tbsp chicken stock**
**1 tsp salt**
**1 pinch pepper**
**1 tsp sugar**
**2 tsp cornflour**
**1 small tin diced pineapple (5 oz/ 150 g)**

Preparation time: 15 minutes
Cooking time: 25 minutes
Energy per serving: approx. 1881 kJ/ 448 cal

1 Heat the oil in a wok and roast the walnuts. Remove and place on a kitchen towel to drain off any excess oil.

2 Cut the chicken breasts into strips and brown in the remaining oil on all sides.

3 Mix together the soy sauce, chicken stock, salt, pepper, sugar and the cornflour and add to the chicken.

4 Bring to the boil and leave to simmer on a low flame for 15 minutes.

5 Drain the pineapple cubes using a colander and add to the wok. Stir in the walnuts. Reheat everything and serve hot.

# GUINEA FOWL WITH SAFFRON AND TOMATOES

Serves 4

- 1 guinea fowl
- 1 tsp curry powder
- 2 tbsp soy sauce
- 1 tsp saffron
- 2 tbsp oil
- 3 onions
- 3 cloves of garlic
- 1 chilli pepper
- 2 tsp anchovy paste
- 1 tsp cinnamon
- 1 tsp salt
- 3 bay leaves
- 6 tomatoes

Preparation time: 15 minutes
Cooking time: 90 minutes
Energy per serving: approx. 2004 kJ/ 477 cal

1 Wash and divide the guinea fowl into 6–8 portions.

2 Mix together the curry powder, soy sauce and the saffron and use the mixture to brush on the guinea fowl pieces.

3 Heat the oil in a frying pan and brown the pieces of guinea fowl on all sides.

4 Peel and dice the onions and the garlic. Wash, halve, deseed and chop the chilli. Add everything to the frying pan and cook.

5 Add the anchovy paste, cinnamon, salt and the bay leaves.

6 Skin and coarsely chop the tomatoes. Add them to the pan, bring to the boil and leave to simmer on a low flame for approximately 1 hour. Arrange on plates and serve.

# YELLOW CHICKEN CURRY

**Serves 4**

**1 chicken**

**1 pint (500 ml) coconut milk**

**2 stalks lemon grass**

**2 tbsp peanut butter**

**1 tbsp yellow curry paste**

**1 tsp cinnamon**

**1 tsp ground cardamom**

**lime juice**

**sugar**

**lemon balm for decoration**

Preparation time: 15 minutes
Cooking time: 1 hour
Energy per serving: approx. 1313 kJ/ 312 cal

1 Wash the chicken. Debone and cut into bite sized pieces.

2 Transfer the meat into a large saucepan and add the coconut milk, lemon grass and the peanut butter. Bring to the boil and leave to simmer on a low flame for approximately 40 minutes.

3 Remove the meat and the lemon grass. Stir in the yellow curry paste, cinnamon and the ground cardamom.

4 Bring to the boil and reduce until half the liquid has evaporated. Season with the lime juice and the sugar.

5 Add the chicken again, reheat and arrange on plates. Decorate with the lemon balm and serve.

# Leg of Turkey with Fruit Chutney

1 Wash and thoroughly dry the turkey legs using a kitchen towel.

2 Peel and finely dice the onion and the clove of garlic. Mix together with the vinegar and the curcuma and marinate the turkey legs for approximately 30 minutes.

3 Heat the oil in a frying pan and roast the cinnamon stick and cardamom pods.

4 Remove the turkey legs from the marinade and add to the frying pan. Brown on all sides. Add 4 tbsp of water and continue to cook until the turkey is done.

5 For the chutney deseed the dates and place in a saucepan together with the gooseberries.

6 Wash, halve, deseed and finely chop the chillies. Add to the fruit.

7 Peel and crush the clove of garlic and add to the fruit. Also add the garam masala and the rice wine vinegar. Bring to the boil and continue to simmer on a low flame until the chutney has a thickish consistency.

8 Remove the turkey legs and cut the meat into bite sized pieces. Arrange on plates and serve with the chutney.

**Serves 4**

**2 legs of turkey**

**1 onion**

**1 clove of garlic**

**3 tbsp vinegar**

**1 tsp curcuma**

**oil for frying**

**4 cloves**

**1 cinnamon stick**

**3 cardamom pods**

**For the chutney:**

**7 oz (200 g) fresh dates**

**7 oz (200 g) gooseberries**

**2 chillies**

**1 clove of garlic**

**1 tsp garam masala**

**1/2 pint (250 ml) rice wine vinegar**

Preparation time (excluding marinating time): 15 minutes
Cooking time: 45 minutes
Energy per serving: approx. 1291 kJ/ 307 cal

# Leg of Goose with Lentils

**Serves 4**

**4 goose legs**

**1 tub yoghurt (5 oz/150 g)**

**1 pinch ground cumin**

**1 tbsp ground coriander seeds**

**1 tsp ground curcuma**

**1 tsp chilli sauce**

**1 pinch pepper**

**2 onions**

**1 clove of garlic**

**1 tbsp oil**

**3 cloves**

**3 cardamom stick**

**1 small cinnamon pod**

**lime juice**

**salt**

**For the lentils:**

**10 oz (300 g) red lentils**

**1 tsp salt**

**1 pinch ground coriander seeds**

**1 pinch ground ginger**

**3 cloves**

**2 tbsp garam masala**

**2 onions**

**1 tbsp butter**

Preparation time (excluding marinating time): 15 minutes
Cooking time: 1 hour
Energy per serving: approx. 2671 kJ/ 636 cal

1 Wash and place the legs of goose in a bowl.

2 Whisk the yoghurt until creamy and add the ground cumin, ground coriander seeds, curcuma, chilli sauce and the pepper. Pour over the goose and leave to marinate for approximately 30 minutes.

3 Peel and finely dice the onion and clove of garlic. Heat the oil in a frying pan and sauté the vegetables.

4 Add the cloves, cardamom pods and cinnamon stick and give it a good stir.

5 Add the goose legs including the marinade. Bring to the boil and leave to simmer on a low flame for approximately 40 minutes. Season with the lime juice and salt.

6 Place the lentils and the spices in a saucepan, add sufficient water and cook for approximately 15 minutes.

7 Peel and dice the onions. Melt the butter in a frying pan and brown the onions.

8 Drain the lentils and add to the onions. Reheat and serve together with the legs of goose.

# COLOURFUL POULTRY PLATTER

1 Peel and finely dice the clove of garlic and the fresh ginger. Stir in the salt and pepper.

2 Wash, dry and thinly slice the chicken breasts.

3 Heat the oil in a frying pan and brown the vegetables and the chicken. Cover and leave to cook on a low flame for approximately 10 minutes.

4 Wash and coarsely grate the white cabbage. Peel the carrots and also grate them coarsely. Wash, halve, deseed and cut the green pepper into strips.

5 Add the vegetables to the meat. Pour in half of the chicken stock, bring to the boil and leave to simmer on a low flame for another 20 minutes.

6 Add the rest of the chicken stock 10 minutes before the end. Bring to the boil and add the Chinese egg noodles.

7 Turn up the heat to evaporate any excess liquid, arrange on plates and serve while still hot.

**Serves 4**

**1 clove of garlic**

**1 piece fresh ginger (1 1/4 inches/3 cm)**

**1/2 tsp salt**

**1 pinch pepper**

**13 oz (400 g) chicken breasts**

**2 tbsp oil for frying**

**1/4 white cabbage**

**2 carrots**

**1 green pepper**

**1 pint (500 ml) chicken stock**

**8 oz (250 g) Chinese egg noodles**

Preparation time: 20 minutes
Cooking time: 40 minutes
Energy per serving: approx. 1840 kJ/ 438 cal

# TURKEY FRICASSEE WITH TOFU

**Serves 4**

**1 lb 4 oz (600 g) escalope of turkey**

**2 onions**

**1/2 Chinese cabbage**

**7 oz (200 g) snow peas**

**1 small tin bamboo shoots (sliced)**

**2 tbsp oil**

**1 pinch monosodium glutamate**

**2 tsp soy sauce**

**1 tbsp hoisin sauce**

**5 oz (150 g) tofu**

Preparation time: 20 minutes
Cooking time: 25 minutes
Energy per serving: approx. 1234 kJ/ 294 cal

1 Wash, dry and cut the escalopes of turkey into thin strips.

2 Peel and slice the onions. Wash and cut the Chinese cabbage into finger thick strips.

3 Clean and dry the snow peas using a salad spinner.

4 Drain the bamboo sprouts using a colander.

5 Heat the oil in a frying pan and brown the meat and the onions.

6 Add the Chinese cabbage and snow peas and stir-fry for 10 minutes.

7 Now add the bamboo shoots. Mix the monosodium glutamate, soy sauce and the hoisin sauce and pour into the frying pan.

8 Bring everything to the boil and leave to simmer on a low flame for approximately 5 minutes. Dice the tofu and add to the frying pan. Wait for it to heat up. Arrange everything on plates and serve.

# TURKEY FRICASSEE WITH PEANUTS

Slice 1 lb 4 oz (600 g) escalope of turkey and brown together with 1 tbsp chopped fresh ginger in a frying pan with hot oil. Add 5 tbsp soy sauce and 1/4 pint (125 ml) chicken stock. Stir well, bring to the boil and leave to simmer on a low flame for approximately 20 minutes. Add 3 tbsp peanut butter, some salt and a little sambal oelek and bring to the boil. Arrange the fricassee on plates, sprinkle with chopped peanuts and serve.

**Serves 4**

Preparation time: 20 minutes
Cooking time: 30 minutes
Energy per serving: approx. 1330 kJ/ 316 cal

# TURKEY FRICASSEE WITH CUCUMBER

Slice 1 lb 4 oz (600 g) escalope of turkey and brown in hot oil in a frying pan. Add 2 onions cut into rings and 2 finely chopped cloves of garlic. Wash, dry and halve a cucumber. Deseed using a spoon and slice the cucumber. Add to the frying pan and give it a good stir. Mix together 2 tbsp plum jam, 2 tbsp soy sauce, 2 tbsp hoisin sauce, 2 tsp sugar and a little salt and pour into the frying pan. Bring to the boil, arrange on plates and serve.

**Serves 4**

Preparation time: 20 minutes
Cooking time: 25 minutes
Energy per serving: approx. 977 kJ/ 232 cal

# Stuffed Ginger Chicken

**Serves 4**

**1 onion**

**2 oz (50 g) fresh ginger**

**1 clove of garlic**

**2 tbsp butter**

**8 oz (250 g) mixed minced meat**

**salt**

**1 whole chicken**

**oil for frying**

**approx. 2 pints (1 l) coconut milk**

**red peppers and parsley for decoration**

Preparation time: 20 minutes
Cooking time: 1 1/4 hours
Energy per serving: approx. 1893 kJ/ 450 cal

1 Peel and finely dice the onion, fresh ginger and the clove of garlic.

2 Melt the butter and brown the diced onion, ginger and garlic.

3 Add the minced meat and brown. Season everything with salt.

4 Clean the chicken and stuff it with the meat mixture.

5 Heat the oil in a frying pan and brown the chicken on all sides. Pour in the coconut milk, cover and leave to simmer on a low heat for approximately 1 hour.

6 Remove the chicken and reduce the coconut milk until nice and thick. Arrange on plates, pour on the coconut sauce and garnish with the pepper strips and the parsley.

# Exotic Poultry Ragoût

**Serves 4**

- 3 lb (1 1/2 kg) chicken breasts
- 1 pinch ground cumin
- 1 pinch ground aniseed
- 2 tsp cinnamon
- 1 tbsp ground coriander seeds
- 1 tsp ground cloves
- 1 pinch ground cardamom
- 1 tsp pepper
- 2 tsp salt
- 3 tbsp oil
- 2 tbsp sesame oil for frying
- 7 oz (200 g) freshly grated coconut
- 2 onions
- 1 tbsp lime juice
- 3 tbsp coconut milk
- 3 1/2 oz (100 g) cashew nuts
- 2 tbsp raisins
- 2 tomatoes
- 1 green pepper

Preparation time (excluding marinating time): 15 minutes
Cooking time: 45 minutes
Energy per serving: approx. 3164 kJ/ 753 cal

1 Wash and dice the chicken meat.

2 Mix together the spices and the oil and marinate the chicken in the mixture for approximately 1 hour.

3 Heat the sesame oil in a frying pan and fry the freshly grated coconut.

4 Peel and cut the onions into rings. Add to the coconut and sauté.

5 Add the chicken meat, lime juice and the coconut milk. Bring to the boil and continue to simmer on a low flame for approximately 30 minutes or until the chicken is soft and the sauce quite thick.

6 Stir in the raisins and the cashew nuts 10 minutes before the end. Quarter the tomatoes, slice the green pepper and add to the ragout. Arrange on plates and serve.

# Chicken and Mushroom Casserole

**Serves 4**

**6 dried shiitake mushrooms**

**4 chicken breasts**

**1 piece fresh ginger (1 1/4 inches/3 cm)**

**3 spring onions**

**3 tbsp soy sauce**

**1 tsp sugar**

**2 tbsp peanut oil**

**1 tbsp rice wine**

**1/2 tsp salt**

**8 oz (250 g) rice**

**1/4 pint (125 ml) chicken stock**

Preparation time: 25 minutes
Cooking time: 20 minutes
Energy per serving: approx. 1290 kJ/ 307 cal

1 Cover the shiitake mushrooms with boiling water and leave them to soak until soft.

2 Wash, dry and cut the chicken breasts into bite sized pieces.

3 Peel and finely dice the ginger. Slice the spring onions. Remove the stalks of the mushrooms and cut the caps into strips.

4 Mix the vegetables, diced chicken, soy sauce, sugar, oil, rice wine and the salt.

5 Cook the rice for 15 minutes. Drain, rinse and transfer to an oven-proof dish.

6 Pour the chicken stock over the rice and spoon the meat and vegetable mixture on top. Cover and place on the middle shelf in the oven on gas mark 8 (440 °F or 220 °C) for 20 minutes. Remove and serve.

# DUCK ROLLS IN SWEET AND SOUR SAUCE

1 Wash and dry the duck breasts. Rub the meat with the spices. Heat some oil in a frying pan and brown the meat on all sides.

2 Finely slice the meat and leave to cool.

3 Clean and cut the spring onions into rings.

4 Wash and dry the fresh coriander using a salad spinner and then chop finely.

5 Peel and cut the carrots into small sticks.

6 Soak the leaves of rice paper in hot water.

7 Mix together the vegetables, herbs and the duck meat.

8 Dab the rice paper dry and place the mixture on top. Roll up the leaves and fry in hot peanut oil for approximately 10 minutes.

9 Clean and finely chop the shiitake mushrooms. Wash and finely chop the leek. Peel and finely chop the ginger.

10 Transfer the vegetables into a saucepan. Add the sugar, vinegar, soy sauce, 3 tbsp of water and the cornflour and bring to the boil. Leave to simmer on a medium flame for approximately 10 minutes and serve as a sauce with the duck rolls.

**Serves 4**

**4 skinned breasts of duck**

**1 tsp ground coriander seeds**

**1 tsp black pepper**

**1 tsp salt**

**1 tsp ground cumin**

**oil for frying**

**1 bunch spring onions**

**1 bunch fresh coriander**

**2 carrots**

**4 leaves of rice paper**

**peanut oil for frying**

**For the sauce:**

**4 shiitake mushrooms**

**2 tbsp pickled ginger**

**1/2 leek**

**2 tbsp sugar**

**3 tbsp vinegar**

**3 tbsp soy sauce**

**2 tbsp cornflour**

Preparation time: 40 minutes
Cooking time: 30 minutes
Energy per serving: approx. 1968 kJ/ 468 cal

# PHILIPPINE POULTRY PLATTER

**Serves 4**

**1 1/2 lb (750 g) chicken meat**

**1/2 pint (250 ml) vinegar**

**1 tbsp soy sauce**

**salt**

**pepper**

**1 clove of garlic**

**oil for frying**

**1 pint (500 ml) coconut milk**

**1 tin pineapple cubes (8 oz/225 g)**

**parsley for decoration**

Preparation time: (excluding marinating time): 15 minutes
Cooking time: 45 minutes
Energy per serving: approx. 1134 kJ/ 270 cal

1 Wash, dry and slice the chicken.

2 Mix together the vinegar, soy sauce, salt and pepper and pour over the chicken slices. Peel, crush and add the garlic. Leave everything to marinate for 30 minutes.

3 Transfer the chicken and the marinade into a saucepan, bring to the boil and leave to simmer on a low flame for approximately 15 minutes.

4 Drain the chicken using a sieve. Heat the oil in a frying pan and brown the chicken on all sides.

5 Now pour in the coconut milk and continue to simmer for a while until it thickens somewhat.

6 Drain the pineapple using a sieve and add to the meat. Reheat, arrange on plates and decorate with the parsley. Serve.

# CRISPY QUAILS WITH BROCCOLI SALAD

**Serves 4**

**8 plucked and gutted quails**

**2 pints (1 l) chicken stock**

**oil for frying**

**1 piece fresh ginger (1 1/4 inches/3 cm)**

**2 spring onions**

**2 tbsp peanut oil**

**1 tbsp rice wine**

**2 tbsp soy sauce**

**1 tbsp vegetable stock**

**1 tsp brown sugar**

**2 tsp cornflour**

**For the salad:**

**1 lb (500 g) broccoli**

**2 tbsp light soy sauce**

**2 tbsp rice wine**

**2 tbsp sesame oil**

**salt**

**1 tbsp sugar**

Preparation time: 20 minutes
Cooking time: 45 minutes
Energy per serving: approx. 2457 kJ/ 585 cal

1 Wash the quails and simmer in the chicken stock for approximately 15 to 20 minutes. Remove and leave to drain.

2 Heat sufficient oil in a frying pan to brown the quails well on all sides. Remove and leave to drain. Put to one side and keep warm.

3 Peel and finely chop the fresh ginger. Clean and slice the spring onions. Sauté both in hot peanut oil.

4 Mix together the rice wine, soy sauce, vegetable stock, sugar and the cornflour and pour over the spring onions and ginger. Bring to the boil and serve as sauce to the quails.

5 For the salad wash and divide the broccoli into florets. Blanch the broccoli in slightly salted water for approximately 2 minutes. Remove, leave to dry and cool.

6 Mix together the rice wine, soy sauce, oil, salt and sugar and pour over the broccoli. Serve together with the quails.

# Pheasant with Spinach Leaves

**Serves 4**

**1 plucked and gutted pheasant**

**1 tbsp sesame seeds**

**1 onion**

**1 clove of garlic**

**1 tsp pepper**

**4 tbsp soy sauce**

**1 tsp sugar**

**1 tbsp sesame oil**

**2 lb (1 kg) spinach leaves**

**oil for frying**

Preparation time (excluding marinating time): 30 minutes
Cooking time: 1 1/2 hours
Energy per serving: approx. 2458 kJ/ 585 cal

1 Wash, dry and debone the pheasant. Cut the meat into slices, then place in a shallow bowl and sprinkle with the sesame seeds.

2 Peel and finely dice the onion and the clove of garlic. Mix together with the pepper, soy sauce, sugar and the sesame oil and pour the mixture over the meat. Leave to marinate for approximately 30 minutes.

3 Blanch the spinach leaves in manageable portions in boiling water for 2 minutes. Remove, leave to drain and coarsely chop the spinach.

4 Heat the oil in a frying pan and brown the pieces of pheasant. Add a little of the marinade, bring to the boil and leave to simmer on a low heat for approximately 1 hour.

5 Finally reduce the liquid and add the spinach. Reheat while stirring continuously and serve hot.

# ROAST DUCK YUNNAN STYLE

1 Wash and dry the duck.

2 Clean and finely slice the spring onions. Peel and crush the cloves of garlic. Mix together with the bean paste, cinnamon, monosodium glutamate, sugar, pepper, rice wine, salt and the chicken stock. Transfer everything into a saucepan and cook on a high heat for approximately 2 minutes.

3 Stuff the mixture into the duck and secure with a small skewer or a couple of wooden toothpicks.

4 Mix together the soy sauce, honey and 1 tbsp of water and brush onto the duck.

5 Place the duck in a roasting tin, cover with a tight fitting lid and place on the middle shelf in the oven. Roast the duck on gas mark 7 (450 °F or 225 °C) for approximately 50 minutes. Remove the lid and continue to roast the duck, braising it every now and then, until nice and crispy.

6 Heat the sesame oil in a frying pan, add the bean paste, sugar and 1/4 pint (125 ml) of water and reduce until the sauce is thickened.

7 Remove the duck from the roasting tin, carve and serve with the sauce.

**Serves 4**

**11 duck (3 lb/1 1/2 kg)**

**1 bunch spring onions**

**2 cloves of garlic**

**1 tbsp bean paste**

**1 tsp cinnamon**

**1 tsp monosodium glutamate**

**1 tbsp brown sugar**

**1 pinch black pepper**

**2 tbsp rice wine**

**2 tsp salt**

**1/2 pint (250 ml) chicken stock**

**2 tbsp soy sauce**

**1 tbsp honey**

**For the sauce:**

**2 tbsp sesame oil**

**6 tbsp sweet bean paste**

**2 tbsp sugar**

Preparation time: 15 minutes
Cooking time: 2 hours
Energy per serving: approx. 2512 kJ/ 598 cal

# EGG RICE WITH CHICKEN

**Serves 4**

**13 oz (400 g) rice**

**salt**

**10 oz (300 g) chicken breast fillets**

**7 oz (200 g) radish**

**1 carrot**

**7 oz (200 g) shiitake mushrooms**

**3/4 pint (375 ml) fish stock**

**6 tbsp soy sauce**

**4 tbsp sake**

**6 eggs**

Preparation time: 15 minutes
Cooking time: 50 minutes
Energy per serving: approx. 1685 kJ/ 401 cal

1 Cook the rice in sufficient slightly salted water for approximately 20 minutes. Drain and rinse under the running cold tap.

2 Wash and cut the chicken breasts into finger thick slices.

3 Peel the radish and cut into thick slices. Peel the carrot and cut into strips. Clean and slice the shiitake mushrooms.

4 Mix together the fish stock, soy sauce and sake and bring to the boil. Add the meat and vegetables, bring to the boil and leave to simmer on a low heat for 20 minutes. Drain using a sieve, making sure to preserve the cooking liquid.

5 Transfer the meat and the vegetables into a frying pan or wok and add just enough cooking liquid so that the base is covered.

6 Whisk the eggs and pour over the contents of the pan. Leave to set on a medium heat.

7 Transfer the rice into a bowl and cover with the rest of the hot cooking liquid. Place the egg, meat and vegetable mixture on top and serve.

# Turkey Aubergine Casserole

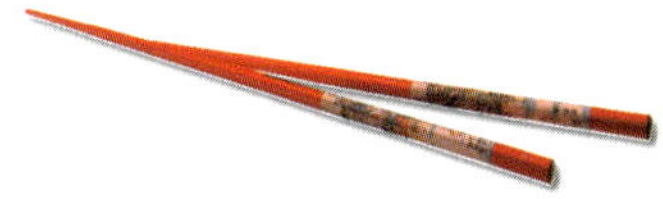

1 Peel and dice the potatoes and cook in slightly salted water for approximately 15 minutes.

2 Peel and crush the cloves of garlic. Peel and finely dice the onions.

3 Peel and finely chop the fresh ginger. Wash and dry the mint using a salad spinner. Then chop finely.

4 Mix together the garlic, onions, ginger, mint, garam masala, chilli sauce, salt and the vinegar until you have a smooth paste.

5 Wash and cut the turkey breasts into largish cubes. Place in a bowl, add half the spice mixture and leave to marinate for approximately 30 minutes.

6 Heat the oil in a frying pan and fry the other half of the spice paste.

7 Wash and slice the aubergines. Transfer to the frying pan, add the curcuma and cook for approximately 5 minutes.

8 Add the meat and continue to cook for another 10 minutes. Pour in 1 pint (500 ml) of water, bring to the boil and leave to simmer on a low heat for approximately 30 minutes.

9 Add the potatoes and reheat everything. Arrange the turkey and aubergine casserole on plates and serve.

**Serves 4**

**10 oz (300 g) potatoes**

**salt**

**3 cloves of garlic**

**2 onions**

**1 piece fresh ginger (1 1/4 inches/3 cm)**

**1/2 bunch fresh mint**

**2 tsp garam masala**

**1/2 tsp chilli sauce**

**1 tsp salt**

**2 tbsp vinegar**

**1 1/2 lb (750 g) turkey breast**

**oil for frying**

**2 aubergines**

**1/2 tsp curcuma**

Preparation time (excluding marinating time): 20 minutes
Cooking time: 1 hour
Energy per serving: approx. 1370 kJ/ 326 cal

# Lemon Spring Chicken

**Serves 4**

**1 spring chicken**
**10 oz (300 g) yoghurt**
**2 tsp chilli powder**
**1 tsp black peppercorns**
**1 tsp chilli sauce**
**4 tbsp vinegar**
**2 tsp ground ginger**
**2 tsp garam masala**
**3 tbsp lemon juice**
**3 cloves of garlic**
**1/2 papaya**
**oil for frying**
**lemon slice for decoration**

Preparation time (excluding marinating time): 20 minutes
Cooking time: 45 minutes
Energy per serving: approx. 1456 kJ/ 346 cal

1 Wash, dry and divide the spring chicken into 6 to 8 portions. Place in a shallow bowl.

2 Whisk the yoghurt until creamy and add the chilli powder, peppercorns, chilli sauce, vinegar, ground ginger, garam masala and the lemon juice. Mix well.

3 Peel and crush the cloves of garlic. Peel the papaya, put into the blender and purée. Add everything to the yoghurt mixture. Pour the marinade over the meat and leave to steep overnight.

4 The following day remove the meat, leave to drain and fry until cooked and golden brown on all sides.

5 Arrange the lemon spring chicken on plates, garnish with the lemon slices and serve.

# Chilli Spring Chicken

Fry 2 onions cut into onion rings, 2 crushed cardamom pods, 1 cinnamon stick, 1 tbsp chopped ginger and 1 tbsp ground cumin. Add 2 skinned tomatoes and give it a good stir. Rub the spring chicken with 3 crushed chillies, divide into 6 to 8 portions and add to the frying pan. Fry a little longer before pouring in 1/2 pint (250 ml) of chicken stock. Bring to the boil and continue to simmer on a low heat until the spring chicken is properly cooked.

**Serves 4**
Preparation time: 15 minutes
Cooking time: 45 minutes
Energy per serving: approx. 1167 kJ/ 278 cal

# Coconut Spring Chicken

Fry 2 tbsp freshly grated coconut in 2 tbsp of oil. Remove from the frying pan. Divide the spring chicken into 6 to 8 portions and fry until golden brown on all sides. Sprinkle with 1 pinch of saffron, 1 pinch of chilli powder, 1 tbsp ground coriander seeds, salt and 2 tsp ground ginger. Pour in 1 pint (500 ml) coconut milk, bring to the boil and continue to simmer on a low heat until the chicken is properly cooked. Arrange on plates, sprinkle with the grated coconut and serve.

**Serves 4**
Preparation time: 15 minutes
Cooking time: 45 minutes
Energy per serving: approx. 1365 kJ/ 325 cal

# DUCK BREAST ON BANANA RICE

**Serves 4**

- **1 onion**
- **2 tbsp sesame oil**
- **2 bananas**
- **8 oz (250 g) rice**
- **1 1/2 pints (750 ml) coconut milk**
- **1 tsp salt**
- **4 duck breasts (with skin)**
- **1 tsp cinnamon**
- **1 tsp monosodium glutamate**
- **pepper, salt**
- **1 pinch ground coriander seeds**
- **oil for frying**

Preparation time: 15 minutes
Cooking time: 40 minutes
Energy per serving: approx. 2090 kJ/ 497 cal

1 Peel and finely dice the onion.

2 Heat the oil in a frying pan and sauté the diced onion. Peel, mash and add the bananas.

3 Stir in the rice and continue to cook until it becomes translucent. Pour in the coconut milk, season with salt, bring to the boil and simmer on a low heat for 20 minutes.

4 Wash, dry and rub the duck breasts with the spices.

5 Heat the oil in a frying pan. Cook until done and the meat is brown and the skin crispy.

6 Arrange the banana rice on plates. Slice the duck breasts, place on top of the rice and serve.

## TIP

Asian cooking makes frequent use of monosodium glutamate to increase an ingredient's flavour without changing it in any way. Normally the salts of the monosodium glutamate acid are harmless. However, some people are susceptible to this substance and experience an allergic reaction. In this case you should not use monosodium glutamate at all.

# POULTRY FONDUE JAPANESE STYLE

1 Wash and dry the spring chicken. Remove the skin, debone and cut the meat into bite sized pieces. Distribute on platters and put to one side.

2 Wash and cut the vegetables into bite sized pieces.

3 Soak the tongu mushrooms. When ready, squeeze them, remove the stem and cut in half if necessary.

4 Distribute the vegetables on plates and put to one side, too.

5 Mix together the lemon juice, soy sauce and 5 tbsp of water.

6 Peel and finely grate the radish. Transfer into a small bowl.

7 Mix together the chicken stock, sake and the sugar. Pour into a fondue pan and put on the heat. Everyone gets a plate with the vegetables and the meat so that they can cook their food in the stock themselves. You can use the sauce and the radish as dips or accompaniments.

**Serves 4**

**1 spring chicken**

**10 oz (300 g) Chinese cabbage**

**7 oz (200 g) carrots, 10 oz (300 g) leeks, 4 dried tongu mushrooms**

**5 tbsp lemon juice**

**5 tbsp soy sauce**

**10 oz (300 g) radish**

**3 pints (1 1/2 l) chicken stock**

**1 tbsp sake**

**1 tsp sugar**

Preparation time: 25 minutes
Energy per serving: approx. 1707 kJ/ 406 cal

# TERIYAKI POULTRY

**Serves 4**

**1 lb (500 g) chicken or turkey breasts**

**1 piece fresh ginger (3/4 inch/2 cm)**

**3 tbsp soy sauce**

**2 tbsp rice wine**

**1 tsp sugar**

**2 tbsp cornflour**

**oil for frying**

Preparation time (excluding marinating time): 20 minutes
Cooking time: 20 minutes
Energy per serving: approx. 731 kJ/ 174 cal (excluding the side dish)

1 Wash and cut the meat into largish pieces.

2 Peel and finely chop the fresh ginger. Place in a bowl and mix with the soy sauce, rice wine and the sugar to make a sauce.

3 Place the meat in the sauce and leave to marinate for approximately 20 minutes.

4 Remove the meat, drain and cover with the cornflour.

5 Heat the oil and brown the meat.

6 Pour in the marinade and leave to simmer until the meat is properly cooked. Serve ready-made Asian noodles Ayam chicken flavour as an accompaniment.

# CHICKEN LEGS WITH RICE AND PEAS

1 Wash and place the chicken legs into a saucepan with sufficient water. Peel the onion and add to the pot. Bring everything to the boil, skim and leave to simmer on a low flame for approximately 30 minutes.

2 Melt the butter and fry the rice until it becomes translucent. Pour in the chicken stock and bring to the boil.

3 Add the peas and spices to the rice and leave to simmer on a low heat for approximately 20 minutes.

4 Remove the chicken legs from the stock, drain and place in a frying pan with hot oil. Brown on all sides. Arrange on plates, add the rice and serve.

**Serves 4**

- **4 chicken legs**
- **1 onion**
- **2 tbsp butter**
- **8 oz (250 g) rice**
- **1 1/2 pints (750 ml) chicken stock**
- **7 oz (200 g) fresh peas**
- **6 cloves**
- **6 cardamom pods**
- **1/2 cinnamon stick**
- **salt**
- **1/2 tsp cumin**
- **oil for frying**

Preparation time: 15 minutes
Cooking time: 50 minutes
Energy per serving: approx. 1640 kJ/ 390 cal

# Vegetables – the favourite ingredient to a well-balanced diet

The value of crispy, fresh vegetables has been known in Asian cooking for well over 5,000 years – a reason why they are often no more than simply heated up.

# MARINATED VEGETABLES IN RICE PAPER

**Serves 4**

**1 radish**

**7 oz (200 g) carrots**

**1 bunch spring onions**

**2 tbsp vinegar**

**pepper**

**4 tbsp oil**

**1/2 tsp coriander seeds**

**1/2 tsp cumin**

**8 leaves rice paper**

**chives for decoration**

Preparation time (excluding marinating time): 20 minutes
Cooking time: 20 minutes
Energy per serving: approx. 845 kJ/ 201 cal

1 Clean, peel and finely slice the radish. Peel and finely slice the carrots. Clean and slice the spring onions.

2 Mix together the vinegar, pepper, oil, coriander seeds and the cumin to make the marinade.

3 Pour over the vegetables and leave to marinate for approximately 1 hour.

4 Soak the rice paper in cold water for approximately 20 minutes.

5 Remove the vegetables and place onto the leaves of rice paper. Fold up the edges and roll up similar to spring rolls.

6 Arrange the vegetable rolls on plates, garnish with the chives and serve.

# TAMIL VEGETABLE RICE

**Serves 4**

**12 oz (375 g) basmati rice**

**salt**

**1 bay leaf, 2 cloves**

**1 tsp curcuma**

**1 cinnamon stick**

**2 oz (50 g) raisins**

**1 aubergine**

**3 tomatoes**

**5 oz (150 g) carrots**

**1 green pepper**

**2 tbsp oil**

**8 oz (250 g) button mushrooms**

**1 tbsp rice wine**

**1 tbsp fish sauce**

**sugar**

**fresh mint for decoration**

Preparation time: 15 minutes
Cooking time: 45 minutes
Energy per serving: approx. 1058 kJ/ 252 cal

1 Cook the rice with the bay leaf, cloves, curcuma and the cinnamon stick in sufficient slightly salted water for 20 minutes.

2 Drain and stir in the raisins.

3 Wash and coarsely dice the aubergine.

4 Skin, deseed and slice the tomatoes. Peel the carrots and grate coarsely. Halve, deseed and cut the green pepper into strips.

5 Heat the oil in a frying pan and sauté the vegetables. Clean and – depending on their size – cut the button mushrooms into bite sized pieces. Add to the frying pan.

6 Mix together the rice wine, fish sauce and the sugar and pour into the frying pan. Bring to the boil and leave to simmer on a low flame for approximately 15 minutes.

7 Add the rice, reheat, arrange on plates and decorate with the fresh mint. Serve.

# SWEET AND SOUR BROCCOLI

**Serves 4**

**1 lb (500 g) broccoli**

**3 tbsp sesame seeds**

**2 tbsp sugar**

**1/4 pint (125 ml) vinegar**

**1 tbsp soy sauce**

**1 tbsp bean paste**

**1 pinch monosodium glutamate**

**ready-made Asian noodles Soto Ayam flavour as an accompaniment**

Preparation time: 10 minutes
Cooking time (excluding marinating time): 10 minutes
Energy per serving: approx. 617 kJ/147 cal

1 Clean the broccoli and divide into florets. Blanch in boiling water for approximately 2 minutes. Remove and drain.

2 Roast the sesame seeds in a frying pan without any oil or margarine. Crush finely in a mortar.

3 Mix together the sugar, vinegar, crushed sesame seeds, soy sauce, bean paste and the monosodium glutamate.

4 Pour the marinade over the broccoli and leave to steep for approximately 1 hour. Then remove the broccoli, leave to drain and serve with ready-made Asian noodles Soto Ayam flavour.

# MIXED VEGETABLES WITH COCONUT MILK

1 Wash and finely slice the white cabbage.

2 Clean the beans. Chop if necessary or desired.

3 Divide the cauliflower into florets. Peel and finely slice the carrots.

4 Wash and drain the soy bean sprouts. Halve, deseed and cut the green pepper into diamond shaped pieces.

5 Peel and finely chop the onions and cloves of garlic.

6 Place everything into a large sauce pan, add the chicken stock and spices and bring to the boil. Leave to simmer on a low heat for approximately 15 minutes.

7 Pour in the coconut milk, stirring continuously. Reheat, arrange on plates and serve.

**Serves 4**

**3 1/2 oz (100 g) white cabbage**

**3 1/2 oz (100 g) green beans**

**3 1/2 oz (100 g) cauliflower**

**3 1/2 oz (100 g) carrots**

**3 1/2 oz (100 g) soy bean sprouts**

**1 green pepper**

**2 onions**

**2 cloves of garlic**

**1/4 pint (125 ml) chicken stock**

**salt, black pepper**

**1 tsp ground ginger**

**1 tsp ground coriander seeds**

**2 tsp soy sauce**

**1/2 pint (250 ml) coconut milk**

Preparation time: 20 minutes
Cooking time: 20 minutes
Energy per serving: approx. 324 kJ/77 cal

# Vegetable and Tofu Ragoût

- **Serves 4**
- **1/2 Chinese cabbage**
- **1 aubergine**
- **1 spring onion**
- **2 cloves of garlic**
- **3 tbsp peanut oil**
- **10 oz (300 g) tofu**
- **salt**
- **pepper**
- **2 tsp chilli sauce**
- **2 tbsp soy sauce**
- **2 tsp cornflour**
- **1 tsp sugar**
- **1/2 bunch chives**

Preparation time: 20 minutes
Cooking time: 15 minutes
Energy per serving: approx. 711 kJ/169 cal

1 Clean the Chinese cabbage and remove the stump. Cut the cabbage into finger thick slices.

2 Wash and cut the aubergine into largish cubes.

3 Clean and slice the spring onion. Peel and finely chop the cloves of garlic.

4 Heat the oil in a frying pan and sauté the vegetables while stirring continuously.

5 Dice and add the tofu.

6 Mix together the salt, pepper, chilli sauce, soy sauce, cornflour and the sugar and pour into the frying pan. Bring to the boil and leave to simmer on a low flame for approximately 5 minutes.

7 Wash and dry the chives using a salad spinner. Cut into rings. Arrange the vegetable and tofu ragoût on plates, sprinkle with the chives and serve.

# FRIED PEPPERS

1 Mix together the minced beef, soy sauce, pepper and the sesame seeds.

2 Peel, finely chop and add the clove of garlic to the meat.

3 Wash, halve and deseed the peppers. Fill the peppers with the meat mixture.

4 Cover the stuffed peppers with cornflour and then dip into the whisked egg.

5 Heat the sesame oil in a frying pan. Add the stuffed peppers, put on a tight fitting lid and leave to cook on a low heat for approximately 20 minutes.

6 To make the sauce, mix together the soy sauce, sugar and the vinegar. Transfer the stuffed peppers to plates, pour over the sauce and sprinkle with the pine kernels. Serve.

**Serves 4**

**8 oz (250 g) minced beef**

**2 tbsp soy sauce, pepper**

**2 tbsp sesame seeds**

**1 clove of garlic**

**4 long, yellow peppers**

**1 tbsp cornflour**

**1 egg**

**2 tbsp sesame oil**

**For the sauce:**

**1/4 pint (125 ml) soy sauce**

**1 tbsp sugar**

**3 tbsp vinegar**

**1 tbsp chopped pine kernels**

Preparation time: 15 minutes
Cooking time: 30 minutes
Energy per serving: approx. 1429 kJ/ 340 cal

# CAULIFLOWER CURRY

**Serves 4**

**1 piece fresh ginger (3/4 inch/2 cm)**

**1 tbsp peanut oil**

**1 tsp curcuma**

**1 tsp ground coriander seeds**

**1 tsp black pepper-corns**

**1 tbsp curry powder**

**1 cauliflower**

**1/4 pint (125 ml) coconut milk**

Preparation time: 15 minutes
Cooking time: 20 minutes
Energy per serving: approx. 264 kJ/ 63 cal

1 Peel and coarsely grate the ginger.

2 Heat the oil in a frying pan. Sauté the grated ginger together with the spices.

3 Wash and divide the cauliflower into florets.

4 Add the cauliflower florets to the frying pan and give it a good stir. Pour in the coconut milk and simmer for some10 minutes, while stirring continuously. Arrange on plates and serve.

# ONION CUCUMBER CURRY

Heat some oil in a frying pan and add 2 tbsp finely chopped fresh ginger and 2 tbsp curry powder. Give it a good stir and add 1 finely chopped chilli pepper and 3 coarsely diced onions. Peel, deseed and chop 2 cucumbers into largish pieces. Add to the frying pan, give it a good stir and pour in 1/2 pint (250 ml) of coconut milk. Bring to the boil and leave to simmer on a low flame for approximately 10 minutes. Serve on a bed of rice.

**Serves 4**
Preparation time: 15 minutes
Cooking time: 20 minutes
Energy per serving: approx. 318 kJ/75 cal

# AUBERGINE CURRY

Wash and coarsely chop 2 aubergines. Heat some oil in a frying pan and add 2 finely diced onions and 1 chopped clove of garlic. Sauté the vegetables. Add 1 tbsp curry powder and 1 tsp garam masala and give it a good stir. Add the aubergines and sauté. Stir in 1 tsp tomato purée, bring to the boil and leave to simmer on a low flame for approximately 10 minutes.

**Serves 4**
Preparation time: 15 minutes
Cooking time: 20 minutes
Energy per serving: approx. 298 kJ/71 cal

# STEWED WHITE CABBAGE

■ **Serves 4**

**3 1/2 oz (100 g) soy bean sprouts**

**7 oz (200 g) white cabbage**

**6 cloves of garlic**

**3 tbsp fat**

**1 tsp fish sauce**

**1 tsp soy sauce**

**sugar**

**pepper**

Preparation time: 15 minutes
Cooking time: 15 minutes
Energy per serving: approx. 513 kJ/122 cal

1 Wash and dry the soy bean sprouts using a salad spinner.

2 Clean and finely slice the white cabbage. Blanch in boiling water for approximately 1 minute. Drain and put to one side.

3 Peel and finely chop the cloves of garlic. Heat the fat in a frying pan and sauté the garlic. Add the cabbage and the soy bean sprouts and stir-fry for 5 minutes.

4 Add the fish sauce and the soy sauce as well as the spices. Continue to cook for another 5 minutes. Transfer onto plates and serve.

## TIP

You can use Chinese cabbage or other sorts of cabbages instead of the strongly flavoured white cabbage. Pak choi (or bok choy in Chinese) is also ideally suited to this recipe. It is mainly grown in the Netherlands although it is increasingly becoming available in the UK, too. The crispy dark green leaves are interlaced with broad soft veins and the vegetable has a pleasant mild flavour.

# FRIED MASHED PEAS

1 Soak the peas in sufficient cold water and leave overnight.

2 Peel and dice the shallot. Peel the fresh ginger.

3 Drain the peas and place in the blender. Add the ginger and the shallot and pour in 2 tbsp of water. Purée everything.

4 Season with salt and sugar.

5 Heat 4 tbsp of the oil in a frying pan, add the pea mash and cook for approximately 5 minutes while stirring continuously. Spread the purée a little less than 1/2 inch (1 cm) thick on a tray and cut into diamond shapes.

6 Cut the potatoes into sticks and brown in the remaining 2 tbsp of oil.

7 Mix together 1/2 pint (250 ml) of water, 1 tsp caraway seeds, ground coriander, ground ginger, curry powder, paprika and the yoghurt.

8 Roast the garam masala in the frying pan. Add the seasoned yoghurt mixture and bring to the boil.

9 Add the potatoes and cook for approximately 10 minutes. Add the pea mash and reheat.

10 Roast the rest of the caraway seeds and the fennel seeds in a frying pan without any oil or margarine before crushing the seeds in a mortar. Arrange the mashed pea, pour over the melted butter and sprinkle with the crushed seeds and the chopped fresh coriander. Serve.

**Serves 4**

- **8 oz (250 g) yellow peas**
- **1 shallot**
- **1 piece fresh ginger (1/2 inch/1 cm)**
- **salt, sugar**
- **7 tbsp oil**
- **1 lb (500 g) potatoes**
- **2 tsp caraway seeds**
- **1 tsp ground coriander seeds**
- **1 tsp ground ginger**
- **1 tsp curry powder**
- **1 tsp paprika**
- **10 oz (300 g) yoghurt**
- **1 tsp garam masala**
- **1 tsp fennel seeds**
- **1 oz (20 g) butter**
- **1 bunch fresh coriander**

Preparation time (excluding soaking time): 15 minutes
Cooking time: 20 minutes
Energy per serving: approx. 1583 kJ/ 377 cal

# Vegetable Salad

**Serves 4**

**5 oz (150 g) carrots**

**1 cucumber**

**3 1/2 oz (100 g) fresh soy bean sprouts**

**1 tbsp chicken stock**

**4 tbsp vinegar**

**1 tbsp sugar**

**1 tbsp soy sauce**

**1 tsp rice wine**

**fresh coriander for decoration**

Preparation time: 15 minutes
Cooking time (excluding marinating time): 10 minutes
Energy per serving: approx. 205 kJ/49 cal

1 Clean, peel and cut the carrots into smallish sticks.

2 Peel and slice the cucumber. If you prefer, you can dispense with the peeling.

3 Wash and drain the soy bean sprouts.

4 Mix together the chicken stock, vinegar, soy sauce and the rice wine.

5 Pour the dressing over the vegetables, toss well and leave to steep for approximately 30 minutes.

6 Arrange the salad on plates, decorate with the fresh coriander and serve.

# STIR FRIED BEANS

1 Mix together the soy sauce, potato starch, 1/4 pint (125 ml) of water, salt and the sugar.

2 Pour boiling water over the dried Chinese mushrooms and leave to soak. When ready remove the stalk and cut the mushrooms into strips.

3 Peel and finely grate the fresh piece of ginger.

4 Wash and – if desired – cut the beans to a bite sized length. Peel and finely chop the cloves of garlic.

5 Heat the oil in a frying pan and sauté the garlic and the grated ginger.

6 Add the beans and the mushrooms and stir-fry for approximately 2 minutes.

7 Pour in the sauce, bring to the boil and leave to simmer on a low flame for approximately 5 minutes. Arrange on plates and serve.

**Serves 4**

**2 tbsp soy sauce**

**2 tsp potato starch**

**1 pinch salt**

**1/2 tsp sugar**

**12 dried Chinese mushrooms**

**1 piece fresh ginger (3/4 inch/2 cm)**

**1 lb (500 g) green beans**

**6 cloves of garlic**

**4 tbsp oil**

Preparation time: 15 minutes
Cooking time: 15 minutes
Energy per serving: approx. 697 kJ/166 cal

# STEAMED CELERY

**Serves 4**

**2 spring onions**

**1 piece fresh ginger (3/4 inch/2 cm)**

**1 lb (500 g) celery**

**2 tbsp oil**

**salt**

**1 pinch monosodium glutamate**

**pepper**

**1/2 tsp sugar**

**1 tbsp sake**

**3/8 pint (200 ml) chicken stock**

**1 tsp cornflour**

Preparation time: 15 minutes
Cooking time: 20 minutes
Energy per serving: approx. 483 kJ/115 cal

1 Clean and finely chop the spring onions.

2 Peel and finely grate the fresh ginger.

3 Wash and cut the celery stalks into bite sized pieces.

4 Heat the oil in a frying pan and sauté the vegetables.

5 Add the spices and the sake and give it a good stir. Pour in the chicken stock, add the cornflour and bring to the boil. Continue to simmer for 10 minutes.

6 Arrange the vegetables on plates and serve.

# FRIED CARROTS

**Serves 4**

**6 large carrots**

**2 red chillies**

**2 onions**

**1 clove of garlic**

**8 oz (250 g) mixed minced meat**

**2 tbsp sesame seeds**

**3 tbsp soy sauce**

**pepper**

**1 tbsp sesame oil**

**3 tbsp sugar, salt**

Preparation time: 15 minutes
Cooking time: 25 minutes
Energy per serving: approx. 1360 kJ/ 324 cal

1 Peel and dice the carrots. Put to one side.

2 Wash, halve, deseed and finely chop the chillies. Peel and finely dice the onions. Peel and finely chop the clove of garlic.

3 Mix together the minced meat, chillies, onions, garlic, sesame seeds and the soy sauce and season with the pepper.

4 Heat the oil in a frying pan and brown the meat, stirring well.

5 Add the carrots, sauté and pour in 5 tbsp of water. Add the sugar and salt to taste. Bring to the boil and leave to simmer on a low flame for approximately 15 minutes. Arrange on plates and serve.

# SWEETS AND DESSERTS – SEDUCTIVE AND ALMOST TOO BEAUTIFUL TO BE EATEN

The typical dessert as we know it does not really exist in Asia. Sweets are usually part and parcel of a planned menu and serve to neutralise your taste buds. Only if tongue and palate are "well chilled" are they ready for the next taste explosion.

# DATE COOKIES

**Serves 4**

**1 cup flour**

**1 tsp baking powder**

**1/2 tsp salt**

**3 tbsp sugar**

**6 fresh dates**

**oil for frying**

Preparation time: 20 minutes

Cooking time: 15 minutes

Energy per serving: approx. 879 kJ/209 cal

1 Mix together the flour, baking powder, salt and the sugar. Add just enough water to get a smooth dough.

2 Sprinkle some flour over your working surface and roll out the dough until it is about 1/5 inch (1/2 cm) thick. Use a coffee cup to cut the dough into circles.

3 Finely chop the dates. Spoon a little of the fruit onto the centre of each circle and press into the dough. Heat the oil in a frying pan and fry the cakes until golden yellow Serve hot.

# Pudding of the "Eight Delights"

**Serves 4**

**5 oz (150 g) short grain rice**

**2 oz (50 g) sugar**

**3 tbsp butter**

**5 oz (150 g) mixed candied fruit (8 different fruit)**

**slices of apple and lemon balm for decoration**

Preparation time: 20 minutes
Cooking time: 35 minutes
Energy per serving: approx. 1192 kJ/ 284 cal

1 Add the short grain rice and 3/8 pint (200 ml) of water to a saucepan, bring to the boil and leave to simmer on a low flame for approximately 15 minutes.

2 Leave to cool and stir in the butter and the sugar.

3 Chop the candied fruits and place on the base of an oven-proof dish. Spread the rice on top and cook in a water bath for approximately 30 minutes.

4 Leave the pudding to cool before turning it out onto a plate. Decorate with the apple slices and the lemon balm and serve.

# CHINESE NEW YEAR FRITTERS

**Serves 4**

**1 lb (500 g) flour**

**fresh yeast**

**1 packet vanilla sugar**

**3 oz (80 g) sugar**

**1 pinch salt**

**3 oz (80 g) lukewarm butter**

**2 eggs**

**1/2 pint (250 ml) lukewarm milk**

**strips of grease proof paper with New Year wishes**

**1 egg white**

**oil for frying**

**a little icing sugar**

Preparation time: 35 minutes
Cooking time: 20 minutes
Energy per serving: approx. 3181 kJ/ 757 cal

1 Sieve the flour into a bowl. Make a little dip in the middle to crumble the yeast in.

2 Add the vanilla sugar, sugar, salt, butter and the eggs and place around the edges.

3 Pour in the lukewarm milk and knead until you have a nice and pliable dough. Knead the yeast dough and leave to rise in a warm place for approximately 30 minutes.

4 Sprinkle some flour onto your working surface and roll out the dough to a thickness of 1/2 inch (1 cm). Use a cup to cut the dough into circles.

5 Place a strip of the grease-proof paper in the middle of each circle. Brush the edges with the egg white and press firmly together to form small parcels.

6 Place in a deep fryer and cook until golden yellow. Leave to cool. You can sprinkle on some icing sugar if you like.

# INDONESIAN SAGO

1 Soak the sago in cold water for approximately 12 hours. It is best left overnight.

2 The next day place the sago, sugar, 3 cups of water, vanilla essence, salt and the desiccated coconut into a saucepan and bring to the boil. Continue to simmer on a low flame for approximately 15 minutes.

3 Wash the lemon balm, dry it using a salad spinner and chop finely. Preserve a couple of leaves for decoration.

4 Stir the chopped lemon balm into the sago and transfer to a bowl. Garnish with the cocktail cherries and the lemon balm and serve.

**Serves 4**

**8 oz (250 g) sago**

**1/2 cup sugar**

**1 tsp vanilla essence**

**a few drops green food colouring**

**1 pinch salt**

**1 tsp desiccated coconut**

**1 sprig lemon balm**

**cocktail cherries for decoration**

Preparation time (excluding soaking time): 10 minutes
Cooking time: 20 minutes
Energy per serving: approx. 1287 kJ/ 306 cal

# CARROT AND PUMPKIN HALVA

**Serves 4**

**8 oz (250 g) carrots**

**8 oz (250 g) pumpkin**

**1/4 cup milk**

**2 tbsp butter**

**1 cup brown sugar**

**1 pinch saffron**

**2 cloves**

**4 tbsp raisins**

**4 cardamom pods**

**1 tbsp sliced almonds**

**2 tsp desiccated coconut**

**sprigs of fresh mint for decoration**

Preparation time: 15 minutes
Cooking time: 20 minutes
Energy per serving: approx. 1299 kJ/ 309 cal

1 Clean, peel and finely grate the carrots. Do the same with the pumpkin.

2 Place the vegetables into a saucepan, pour over the milk and bring to the boil. Continue to simmer on a low flame until it takes on a firm consistency.

3 Melt the butter in a frying pan and fry the mixture together with the sugar and the saffron until golden brown.

4 Wash the raisins and place into a saucepan. Add a little water and bring to the boil. Drain using a sieve and stir into the halva. Also add the cardamom pods, sliced almonds and the desiccated coconut.

5 Transfer the mixture into a bowl and leave to cool. Decorate with the fresh mint and serve.

# COCONUT WAFFLES WITH TEA ICE CREAM

1 Mix together the flour, coconut milk, eggs, sugar and 2 tbsp of water to make a smooth dough. Add the lemon juice. Put the dough aside and leave to rest for approximately 30 minutes.

2 It is best to make the ice cream the day before. To do so, pour 3 1/2 fl oz (100 ml) boiling water over the jasmine tea and leave to brew for 5 minutes.

3 Strain the tea and leave to cool.

4 Whip the cream until it is stiff and add half the sugar. Stir the other half of the sugar to the egg yolk and give it a good whisk.

5 Transfer the cream into a large bowl and carefully fold into the egg yolk, tea and the orange juice. Place in the freezer and leave overnight.

6 Cook the waffles using a waffle iron.

7 Take the ice cream out of the freezer and scoop out balls. Arrange on plates and add the waffles. Garnish with the lemon balm and serve immediately.

**Serves 4**

**8 oz (250 g) flour**

**1/2 pint (250 ml) coconut milk**

**2 eggs**

**4 oz (125 g) sugar**

**1 tbsp lemon juice**

**oil for frying**

**For the tea ice cream:**

**1 1/2 tsp jasmine tea**

**10 fl oz (300 ml) single cream**

**2 oz (50 g) sugar**

**1 egg yolk**

**2 fl oz orange juice**

**lemon balm for decoration**

Preparation time (excluding freezing time): 30 minutes
Cooking time: 30 minutes
Energy per serving: approx. 2908 kJ/ 692 cal

# LYCHEE FRITTERS

**Serves 4**

**1 large tin lychees (13 oz/380 g)**

**1 oz (30 g) butter**

**2 oz (50 g) sugar**

**1 vanilla pod, split lengthways**

**2 eggs**

**4 oz (125 g) flour**

**1/4 pint (125 ml) cream**

**1 oz (20 g) ground almonds**

**fat for frying**

**sesame seeds for decoration**

Preparation time: 15 minutes
Cooking time: 15 minutes
Energy per serving: approx. 1999 kJ/ 476 cal

1 Drain the lychees using a sieve.

2 Mix together the butter, sugar and the seeds of the vanilla pod and give everything a good whisk.

3 Separate the eggs and whisk the egg whites until stiff.

4 Mix together the egg yolks, flour, cream, ground almonds and the butter to get a smooth dough. Carefully fold into the egg whites.

5 Dip the lychees into the mixture and fry in hot oil until crispy. Sprinkle with the sesame seeds and serve.

# BANANA FRITTERS

Mash four bananas and mix together with 6 oz (175 g) flour, 1 tsp salt and 3 tbsp sugar. Drop little spoonfuls of the mixture into hot fat and fry until crispy and golden brown. Sprinkle with desiccated coconut and serve.

**Serves 4**
Preparation time: 15 minutes
Cooking time: 15 minutes
Energy per serving: approx. 1323 kJ/ 315 cal

# PINEAPPLE FRITTERS

Mix together 2 tbsp flour and one egg and add a little salt. Open a tin of pineapple, drain using a sieve and dip the pineapple slices into the mixture. Heat some oil in a frying pan and fry until they are crispy and take on a golden brown colour. Sprinkle with desiccated coconut and serve.

**Serves 4**
Preparation time: 15 minutes
Cooking time: 15 minutes
Energy per serving: approx. 512 kJ/122 cal

# Index of recipes